ALSO BY MARK STRAND

POETRY

Almost Invisible, 2012

New Selected Poems, 2007

Man and Camel, 2006

Blizzard of One, 1998

Dark Harbor, 1993

Reasons for Moving, Darker, & The Sargentville Notebook, 1992

The Continuous Life, 1990

Selected Poems, 1980

The Late Hour, 1978

The Monument, 1978

The Story of Our Lives, 1973

Darker, 1970

Reasons for Moving, 1968

Sleeping with One Eye Open, 1964

PROSE

The Weather of Words, 2000

Mr. and Mrs. Baby, 1985

TRANSLATIONS

Looking for Poetry, 2002

Travelling in the Family (Poems by Carlos Drummond de Andrade), 1986
(with Thomas Colchie)

The Owl's Insomnia (Poems by Rafael Alberti), 1973

COLLECTED POEMS

COLLECTED POEMS

MARK STRAND

ALFRED A. KNOPF

NEW YORK

2014

THIS IS A BORZOI BOOK
PUBLISHED BY ALFRED A. KNOPF

Copyright © 2014 by Mark Strand

All rights reserved. Published in the United States by Alfred A. Knopf,
a division of Random House, LLC, New York, and in Canada by
Random House of Canada Limited, Toronto, Penguin Random House companies.

www.aaknopf.com/poetry

Knopf, Borzoi Books, and the colophon are
registered trademarks of Random House LLC.

Library of Congress Cataloging-in-Publication Data
Strand, Mark, [date]
[Poems. Collections]
Collected poems / by Mark Strand.
pages cm
ISBN 978-0-385-35251-2 (hardcover)—ISBN 978-0-385-35252-9 (eBook)
I. Title.
PS3569.T69A6 2014
811'.54—dc23   2013049034

Front-of-jacket illustration: *Yes, But* by Saul Steinberg © The Saul Steinberg
Foundation/Artists Rights Society (ARS), New York
Jacket design by Chip Kidd

Manufactured in the United States of America
First Edition

To Jessica, Lucian, and Maricruz

CONTENTS

Reasons for Moving (1968)

Darker (1970)

The Story of Our Lives (1973)

The Late Hour (1978)

The Continuous Life (1990)

Dark Harbor (1993)   317

Blizzard of One (1998)

I

Man and Camel (2006)

One

Almost Invisible (2012)

SLEEPING WITH ONE EYE OPEN

I

EDITOR'S NOTE

Four poems from this volume, published in an edition of 225 copies by Stone Wall Press (Iowa City), were subsequently included in the collection *Reasons for Moving.* Those poems—"The Whole Story," "The Tunnel," "Violent Storm" and "A Reason for Moving" (which was retitled "Keeping Things Whole")—appear in the contents of that second book in the current *Collected Poems.* With the exception of those four poems, the original contents of *Sleeping with One Eye Open* appears here in full.

WHEN THE VACATION IS OVER FOR GOOD

It will be strange
Knowing at last it couldn't go on forever,
The certain voice telling us over and over
That nothing would change,

And remembering too,
Because by then it will all be done with, the way
Things were, and how we had wasted time as though
There was nothing to do,

When, in a flash
The weather turned, and the lofty air became
Unbearably heavy, the wind strikingly dumb
And our cities like ash,

And knowing also,
What we never suspected, that it was something like summer
At its most august except that the nights were warmer
And the clouds seemed to glow,

And even then,
Because we will not have changed much, wondering what
Will become of things, and who will be left to do it
All over again,

And somehow trying,
But still unable, to know just what it was
That went so completely wrong, or why it is
We are dying.

SLEEPING WITH ONE EYE OPEN

Unmoved by what the wind does,
The windows
Are not rattled, nor do the various
Areas
Of the house make their usual racket—
Creak at
The joints, trusses, and studs.
Instead,
They are still. And the maples,
Able
At times to raise havoc,
Evoke
Not a sound from their branches
Clutches.
It's my night to be rattled,
Saddled
With spooks. Even the half-moon
(Half man,
Half dark), on the horizon,
Lies on
Its side casting a fishy light
Which alights
On my floor, lavishly lording
Its morbid
Look over me. Oh, I feel dead,
Folded
Away in my blankets for good, and
Forgotten.
My room is clammy and cold,

Moonhandled
And weird. The shivers
Wash over
Me, shaking my bones, my loose ends
Loosen,
And I lie sleeping with one eye open,
Hoping
That nothing, nothing will happen.

SOMETHING IS IN THE AIR

by which is not meant
what you have been reading
in the papers, or the rumors
you have been spreading,

nor even what you hate to mention:
the plaster cracking in your new house,
the frequent blowing of fuses, the faucets leaking,
the dangerous games of children.

Something is happening
that you can't figure out.
Things have been put in motion.
Something is in the air.

It is there in the mix-up
when the newscaster flubs his lines.
Or in the trembling of a loser's hand
as he picks up his last card.

On Sundays it is there, in the early afternoon,
while the sun scorches the rooftops
and a half-burnt rag is blown, shadowless,
over the sidewalks and arcades of the dead city.

(AFTER ALBERT ARNOLD SCHOLL)

STANDING STILL

Someone is always carting
The scenery off to the wings.
The thickness of the air,
The darkness that darkens there
Will cover trees and gardens,
Waterfronts and water.

All places that have been
With me will wear away.
I do not lift my voice
Or raise a hand. I am
Not capable of force,
Feeling myself at stake.

And if this movement seems
A kind of theft, well then
I am no more than witness
To a crime. I have no choice.
My role is forced on me,
It keeps my nerves on edge.

I wish I were at ease.
Not sure of where I stand
In the long haul to the wings,
I take things as they come
And let them go. I have
No final say in the matter.

The clicking of switches,
The shuffling behind the scenes
Almost make me suspect
That someone wishes me wrong.
And yet, all that I see
Is level and aboveboard.

How long this will keep up,
I am not sure. My time
Is spent recalling all
I can of what has passed.
I try my best to believe
That nothing is wholly lost.

And I don't get anywhere:
My mind does not support
My pastime well. For all
I know, I might do better
To try picking a time
When all this will be over,

And the last scene arrive,
The lights dim, and I,
Set free from all the places
I have never really been,
Move on beyond the curtains
Of a closing night.

THE MAP

Composed, generally defined
  By the long sharing
Of contours, continents and oceans
  Are gathered in
The same imaginary net.
  Over the map
The portioned air, at times but
  A continuance
Of boundaries, assembles in
  A pure, cloudless
Canopy of artificial calm.
  Lacking the haze,
The blurred edges that surround our world,
  The map draws
Only on itself, outlines its own
  Dimensions, and waits,
As only a thing completed can,
  To be replaced
By a later version of itself.
  Wanting the presence
Of a changing space, my attention turns
  To the world beyond
My window where the map's colors
  Fade into a vague
Afterimage and are lost
  In the variable scene
Of shapes accumulating. I see
  A group of fields
Tend slowly inland from the breaking
  Of the fluted sea,

Black-wing and herring gulls, relaxed
  On the air's currents,
Glide out of sight, and trees,
  Cold as stone
In the gray light of this coastal evening,
  Grow gradually
Out of focus. From the still
  Center of my eyes,
Encompassing in the end nothing
  But their own darkness,
The world spins out of reach. And yet,
  Because nothing
Happens where definition is
  Its own excuse
For being, the map is as it was:
  A diagram
Of how the world might look could we
  Maintain a lasting,
Perfect distance from what is.

OLD PEOPLE ON THE NURSING HOME PORCH

Able at last to stop
And recall the days it took
To get them here, they sit
On the porch in rockers
Letting the faded light
Of afternoon carry them off.

I see them moving back
And forth over the dullness
Of the past, covering ground
They did not know was there,
And ending up with nothing
Save what might have been.

And so they sit, gazing
Out between the trees
Until in all that vacant
Wash of sky, the wasted
Vision of each one
Comes down to earth again.

It is too late to travel
Or even find a reason
To make it seem worthwhile.
Already now, the evening
Reaches out to take
The aging world away.

And soon the dark will come,
And these tired elders feel
The need to go indoors
Where each will lie alone
In the deep and sheepless
Pastures of a long sleep.

NO MAN IS CONTINENT WHO VISITS ISLANDS

You, who desire, night
After night, to cross the sea
In search of islands, letting
Outlandish winds escort you
Where they will, take care.

No good can ever come
Of constant traveling.
Knowing no rest, desire
Will only lead you on
Far out beyond your means.

Islands will take shape
Before you, waves will break
Along the glassy beaches,
Recoil and break again,
O do not go there.

No matter how the birds
Flood the empty air,
The trees tend the shade,
Or flowers rise to meet you,
Do not be taken in.

Set one foot on the shore
And islands will appear
That seem far lovelier
Than those on which you are.
You will be off again.

Your days will turn into
Extensions of the night,
And on the sea's slow drift
Toward what is always new
You will be bound forever.

You who long to escape,
Never again will know
The look of a land laid out,
Where pleasure within bounds
And restraint are commonplace.

SAILING TO ITALY

The old props vanish
  By which we posed
Always, we like to think,
  As ourselves. And the ship,
Bound by a notion of blankness,
  Bears us away.
Aware that to be on deck,
  Above all, means
Desire to heave, or regard
  Without purpose
Porpoises arching themselves,
  We keep our main
Uneasiness below,
  Cramped in the bar,
Where each discovers land
  In common, and tries
Somehow to fabricate
  His missing habits.
We sway this way and that
  In makeshift stances
Until, in rougher water,
  We doubt our sense
Of balance will ever set us
  Straight again.
Finding it hard to stand
  The life on board,
We think ahead, and wonder
  Which will be stranger
When we arrive: ourselves
  Or solid land.

DREAMS

Trying to recall the plot
And characters we dreamed,
 What life was like
Before the morning came,
We are seldom satisfied,
 And even then
There is no way of knowing
If what we know is true.
 Something nameless
Hums us into sleep,
Withdraws, and leaves us in
 A place that seems
Always vaguely familiar.
Perhaps it is because
 We take the props
And fixtures of our days
With us into the dark,
 Assuring ourselves
We are still alive. And yet
Nothing here is certain;
 Landscapes merge
With one another, houses
Are never where they should be,
 Doors and windows
Sometimes open out
To other doors and windows,
 Even the person
Who seems most like ourselves
Cannot be counted on,
 For there have been

Too many times when he,
Like everything else, has done
   The unexpected.
And as the night wears on,
The dim allegory of ourselves
   Unfolds, and we
Feel dreamed by someone else,
A sleeping counterpart,
   Who gathers in
The darkness of his person
Shades of the real world.
   Nothing is clear;
We are not ever sure
If the life we live there
   Belongs to us.
Each night it is the same;
Just when we're on the verge
   Of catching on,
A sense of our remoteness
Closes in, and the world
   So lately seen
Gradually fades from sight.
We wake to find the sleeper
   Is ourselves
And the dreamt-of is someone who did
Something we can't quite put
   Our finger on,
But which involved a life
We are always, we feel,
   About to discover.

WINTER IN NORTH LIBERTY

Snow falls, filling
The moonlit fields.
All night we hear
The wind on the drifts
And think of escaping
This room, this house,
The reaches of ourselves
That winter dulls.

Pale ferns and flowers
Form on the windows
Like grave reminders
Of a summer spent.
The walls close in.
We lie apart all night,
Thinking of where we are.
We have no place to go.

II

YOU AND IT

Think what you like, but
It really is the same. Oh,
You can walk around on it
All right and, watching the speed
With which it falls back, fool
Yourself into thinking it changes,

Or, standing with your head
On it, think it above you
With all the grass of summer
Hanging down, mindless
Birds at your feet, your blood
Rushing up to greet your shadow.

But move, and only the angle
It is regarded from changes.
Turn up the stones and they
Reveal what has always been
Uppermost. Put them back?
And you are where you started.

You could go on for years
And never get close at all
To the obvious bottom of it.
A slave to a number of fictions,
You would learn of only your own
Deep-seated simplicity.

Perhaps, when you are tired
You will stretch out on what
Can be thought its own level.
And closing your eyes at last,
Catching the merest fraction
Of sleep, you will know what I mean.

TAKING A WALK WITH YOU

Lacking the wit and depth
That inform our dreams'
Bright landscapes,
This countryside
Through which we walk
Is no less beautiful
For being only what it seems.
Rising from the dyed
Pool of its shade,
The tree we lean against
Was never made to stand
For something else,
Let alone ourselves.
Nor were these fields
And gullies planned
With us in mind.
We live unsettled lives
And stay in a given place
Only long enough to find
We don't belong.
Even the clouds, forming
Noiselessly overhead,
Are cloudy without
Resembling us and, storming
The vacant air,
Don't take into account
Our present loneliness.
And yet, why should we care?

Already we are walking off
As if to say,
We are not here,
We've always been away.

A POEM ON DANCING

They dance now
Wholly in air, it seems,
Enhanced by atmospheres
Of pure decorum.

Rapt in the flow
Of what they wear, we think
Of light improbable rivers
Moving through air.

No strain escorts
Their grace; they dance so well
Their shadows stand and gape
Along the walls,

And we are pleased
To feel our weight cascade
Around our bones and down
Into our chairs,

For we would never
Spend our lives dancing,
Dancing to an unmusical,
Mean end.

WALKING AROUND

Having arrived by the same door
I left, I left again.
I knew my reasons by heart,
And never lost track of where I was going.

To leave and arrive, arrive and leave
Was all I had in mind.
My drives were simple enough——
I walked for the sake of walking around.

The windy sum of my own motion,
I marveled at myself
In passing. I kept in step
With what I was. Oh, I was dashing,

Or thought I was, until I saw
The distance I had to go
And began somehow to suspect
That my past was catching up with me.

I hurried, not wishing to see myself
Leave before I arrived
As, sometimes in my haste
To get back, I have felt myself try.

THE NUDIST COLONY

This is no place that could be described
    Roughly as rough.
The fields, for instance, flowerless and long
    Move away from you
In a graceful, rolling motion only
    To return. And the trees,
That seem so well disguised at first
    In a shimmery cloud
Of leaves, are after all but the heart
    Of their own matter.
Even the simple sunlight, streaming
    Lavishly down,
Has a way of easing its presence, keeping
    No edge for long.
In a place like this, nothing important
    Ever is done.
Days follow each other, blur,
    And combine to form
One long, luminous passage of time.
    Nothing is planned.
No one works and no one is the worse
    For lack of wear.
Sitting under a tree are two
    Old men discussing
In plain speech what neither one
    Could bear to face
Before. And now, behind them, a group
    Of women, wrapped only
In the fabric of their flesh, walk through
    This summer air

With nothing on their minds but how
    It feels. No one
Seems out of place. Even those who were awkward
    And shy at the start
Of their stay, have set the trappings of
    Their past life out
Of sight and learned to be at ease.
    The wind may blow
Harder, the fields may seem more hurried
    In their motions,
The sun may call it a day too soon;
    It makes no difference
As far as the people are concerned.
    For according to them,
Nothing goes on. Nothing at all
    Until after dark.
And about what happens then, not a word
    Ever is said.
Although the person who comes here and stays,
    Learns that everyone,
No matter what, gets dressed for bed.

IN THE MOUNTAINS

Happening to sit,
For no useful reason,
In such a cold, rough terrain,
We see a snowy herringbone of firs
Flush on the nearest mountain,
And are impressed.

But a moment later
We find our gaze has strayed
To a farther, fainter range
Where only rocks break up
The crust of a plainer cloth.
And beyond,

Balanced at the end
Of sight lies a long question
Of what is sky and what is mountain.
Until, by dark, the whole scene
Folds into one simple texture
And we are deep in something else.

For though we stared at mountains
Earlier, the dark has made us
Wonder where we are, and where
We were, and who we are
Thinking of where we were,
And, even, if.

IN MEMORIAM

Give me six lines written by the most honourable of men,
and I will find a reason in them to hang him.

—Richelieu

We never found the last lines he had written,
Or where he was when they found him.
Of his honor, people seem to know nothing.
And many doubt that he ever lived.
It does not matter. The fact that he died
Is reason enough to believe there were reasons.

III

IN THE PRIVACY OF THE HOME

You want to get a good look at yourself. You stand before a mirror, you take off your jacket, unbutton your shirt, open your belt, unzip your fly. The outer clothing falls from you. You take off your shoes and socks, baring your feet. You remove your underwear. At a loss, you examine the mirror. There you are, you are not there.

SUCCESS STORY

Had I known at the outset the climb would be slow, difficult, at times even tedious, I would have chosen to walk the length of one of the local valleys, resigning myself to limited views, low thoughts, and a life that inspired none of the loftier disenchantments.

But how was I to know? The ground seemed level at first, and the walks were wide. Only gradually did I become aware of climbing; the going got rougher, I would be short of breath, pauses were frequent. Often I would have to retrace my steps until I found a more promising route.

I continued through all seasons and can recall how hopeless my venture seemed during those long winter nights and how, during the spring when my determination thawed, I would have to imagine the winter again, the cold, the discomfort.

If there were times I doubted arriving, I know now that my fears were groundless, for here I am, at the peak of my form, feeling the great blue waste of sky circle the scaffold of my achievement. What more is there? I count myself among the blessed. My life is all downhill.

MAKE BELIEVE BALLROOM TIME

Judging from his suit which was excessively drab but expensive, and his speech which was uninflected and precise, I guessed he was a banker, perhaps a lawyer, even a professor in one of the larger, better universities. It never occurred to me that he might be something else until, during a lull in our conversation, he suddenly got up and began dancing. The others at the party, plainly disturbed by this, affected a more intense involvement than was necessary. They spoke loudly, rapidly. But the man continued dancing. And because I recognized what calling, what distant music he obeyed, I envied him.

A KIND OF WEAKNESS

It grows on you. Slowly. Piecemeal. So that you hardly notice it at first. Eventually, of course, you can't miss it. It blossoms. You take to it as you would any natural part of your self. It begins to look beautiful and you spend hours absorbed in the idea of it.

It gets so bad that you spend whole days before one mirror and then another, turning this way and that, getting just the right angle, letting the light fall just so, heightening the effect. You have your friends come in and look. "Love me, love this," you say. And you point.

Everyone talks about it. Gradually it gets out of hand and you can no longer find a way to show it to advantage. You feel fooled. You hate yourself. You cover your mirrors with dark curtains. You refuse to see your friends. Nothing works. It stays. It eats you.

POEM

He sneaks in the back door,
tiptoes through the kitchen,
the living room, the hall,
climbs the stairs, and enters
the bedroom. He leans
over my bed and says he has come
to kill me. The job
will be done in stages.

First, my toenails
will be clipped, then my toes,
and so on until
nothing is left of me.
He takes a small instrument
from his keychain and begins.
I hear *Swan Lake* being played
on a neighbor's hi-fi and start to hum.

How much time passes,
I cannot tell. But when I come to
I hear him say he has reached my neck
and will not be able to continue
because he is tired. I tell him
that he has done enough,
that he should go home and rest.
He thanks me and leaves.

It shall never cease to amaze me
how easily satisfied
some people are.

REASONS FOR MOVING

EATING POETRY

Ink runs from the corners of my mouth.
There is no happiness like mine.
I have been eating poetry.

The librarian does not believe what she sees.
Her eyes are sad
and she walks with her hands in her dress.

The poems are gone.
The light is dim.
The dogs are on the basement stairs and coming up.

Their eyeballs roll,
their blond legs burn like brush.
The poor librarian begins to stamp her feet and weep.

She does not understand.
When I get on my knees and lick her hand,
she screams.

I am a new man.
I snarl at her and bark.
I romp with joy in the bookish dark.

THE ACCIDENT

A train runs over me.
I feel sorry
for the engineer
who crouches down
and whispers in my ear
that he is innocent.

He wipes my forehead,
blows the ashes
from my lips.
My blood steams
in the evening air,
clouding his glasses.

He whispers in my ear
the details of his life—
he has a wife
and child he loves,
he's always been
an engineer.

He talks
until the beam
from someone's flashlight
turns us white.
He stands.
He shakes his jacket out

and starts to run.
The cinders crack
under his boots,
the air is cold
and thick
against his cheeks.

Back home he sits
in the kitchen,
staring at the dark.
His face is flushed,
his hands are pressed
between his knees.

He sees me sprawled
and motionless
beside the tracks
and the faint blooms
of my breath
being swept away;

the fields bend
under the heavy sheets
of the wind
and birds scatter
into the rafters
of the trees.

He rushes
from the house,
lifts the wreckage
of my body in his arms
and brings me back.
I lie in bed.

He puts his head
down next to mine
and tells me
that I'll be all right.
A pale light
shines in his eyes.

I listen to the wind
press hard against the house.
I cannot sleep.
I cannot stay awake.
The shutters bang.
The end of my life begins.

THE MAILMAN

It is midnight.
He comes up the walk
and knocks at the door.
I rush to greet him.
He stands there weeping,
shaking a letter at me.
He tells me it contains
terrible personal news.
He falls to his knees.
"Forgive me! Forgive me!" he pleads.

I ask him inside.
He wipes his eyes.
His dark blue suit
is like an ink stain
on my crimson couch.
Helpless, nervous, small,
he curls up like a ball
and sleeps while I compose
more letters to myself
in the same vein:

"You shall live
by inflicting pain.
You shall forgive."

THE MAN IN THE TREE

I sat in the cold limbs of a tree.
I wore no clothes and the wind was blowing.
You stood below in a heavy coat,
the coat you are wearing.

And when you opened it, baring your chest,
white moths flew out, and whatever you said
at that moment fell quietly onto the ground,
the ground at your feet.

Snow floated down from the clouds into my ears.
The moths from your coat flew into the snow.
And the wind as it moved under my arms, under my chin,
whined like a child.

I shall never know why
our lives took a turn for the worse, nor will you.
Clouds sank into my arms and my arms rose.
They are rising now.

I sway in the white air of winter
and the starling's cry lies down on my skin.
A field of ferns covers my glasses; I wipe them away
in order to see you.

I turn and the tree turns with me.
Things are not only themselves in this light.
You close your eyes and your coat
falls from your shoulders,

the tree withdraws like a hand,
the wind fits into my breath, yet nothing is certain.
The poem that has stolen these words from my mouth
may not be this poem.

THE GHOST SHIP

Through the crowded street
It floats,

Its vague
Tonnage like wind.

It glides
Through the sadness

Of slums
To the outlying fields.

Slowly,
Now by an ox,

Now by a windmill,
It moves.

Passing
At night like a dream

Of death,
It cannot be heard;

Under the stars
It steals.

Its crew
And passengers stare;

Whiter than bone,
Their eyes

Do not
Turn or close.

THE KITE

for Bill and Sandy Bailey

It rises over the lake, the farms,
The edge of the woods,
And like a body without arms
Or legs it swings
Blind and blackening in the moonless air.
The wren, the vireo, the thrush
Make way. The rush
And flutter of wings
Fall through the dark
Like a mild rain.
We cover our heads and ponder
The farms and woods that rim
The central lake.
A barred owl sits on a limb
Silent as bark.
An almost invisible
Curtain of rain seems to come nearer.
The muffled crack and drum
Of distant thunder
Blunders against our ears.

A row of hills appears.
It sinks into a valley
Where farms and woods surround a lake.
There is no rain.
It is impossible to say what form
The weather will take.
We blow on our hands,
Trying to keep them warm,
Hoping it will not snow.
Birds fly overhead.
A man runs by
Holding the kite string.
He does not see us standing dark
And still as mourners under the sullen sky.
The wind cries in his lapels. Leaves fall
As he moves by them.
His breath blooms in the chill
And for a time it seems that small
White roses fill the air,
Although we are not sure.

Inside the room
The curtains fall like rain.
Darkness covers the flower-papered walls,
The furniture and floors,
Like a mild stain.
The mirrors are emptied, the doors
Quietly closed. The man, asleep
In the heavy arms of a chair,
Does not see us
Out in the freezing air
Of the dream he is having.
The beating of wings and the wind
Move through the deep,
Echoing valley. The kite
Rises over the lake,
The farms, the edge of the woods
Into the moonless night
And disappears.
And the man turns in his chair,
Slowly beginning to wake.

THE MARRIAGE

The wind comes from opposite poles,
traveling slowly.

She turns in the deep air.
He walks in the clouds.

She readies herself,
shakes out her hair,

makes up her eyes,
smiles.

The sun warms her teeth,
the tip of her tongue moistens them.

He brushes the dust from his suit
and straightens his tie.

He smokes.
Soon they will meet.

The wind carries them closer.
They wave.

Closer, closer.
They embrace.

She is making a bed.
He is pulling off his pants.

They marry
and have a child.

The wind carries them off
in different directions.

This wind is strong, he thinks
as he straightens his tie.

I like this wind, she says
as she puts on her dress.

The wind unfolds.
The wind is everything to them.

THE WHOLE STORY

—I'd rather you didn't feel it necessary to tell him,
"That's a fire. And what's more, we can't do anything
about it, because we're on this train, see?"

How it should happen this way
I am not sure, but you
Are sitting next to me,
Minding your own business
When all of a sudden I see
A fire out the window.

I nudge you and say,
"That's a fire. And what's more,
We can't do anything about it,
Because we're on this train, see?"
You give me an odd look
As though I had said too much.

But for all you know I may
Have a passion for fires,
And travel by train to keep
From having to put them out.
It may be that trains
Can kindle a love of fire.

I might even suspect
That you are a fireman
In disguise. And then again
I might be wrong. Maybe
You are the one
Who loves a good fire. Who knows?

Perhaps you are elsewhere,
Deciding that with no place
To go you should not
Take a train. And I,
Seeing my own face in the window
May have lied about the fire.

THE BABIES

Let us save the babies.
Let us run downtown.
The babies are screaming.

You shall wear mink
and your hair shall be done.
I shall wear tails.

Let us save the babies
even if we run in rags
to the heart of town.

Let us not wait for tomorrow.
Let us drive into town
and save the babies.

Let us hurry.
They lie in a warehouse
with iron windows and iron doors.

The sunset pink of their skin
is beginning to glow.
Their teeth

poke through their gums
like tombstones.
Let us hurry.

They have fallen asleep.
Their dreams
are infecting them.

Let us hurry.
Their screams rise
from the warehouse chimney.

We must move faster.
The babies have grown into their suits.
They march all day in the sun without blinking.

Their leader sits in a bulletproof car and applauds.
Smoke issues from his helmet.
We cannot see his face:

we are still running.
More babies than ever are locked in the warehouse.
Their screams are like sirens.

We are still running to the heart of town.
Our clothes are getting ragged.
We shall not wait for tomorrow.

The future is always beginning now.
The babies are growing into their suits.
Let us run to the heart of town.

Let us hurry.
Let us save the babies.
Let us try to save the babies.

THE LAST BUS

(Rio de Janeiro, 1966)

It is dark.
A slight rain
dampens the streets.
Nothing moves

in Lota's park.
The palms hang
over the matted grass,
and the voluminous bushes,

bundled in sheets,
billow beside the walks.
The world is out of reach.
The ghosts of bathers rise

slowly out of the surf and turn
high in the spray.
They walk on the beach
and their eyes burn

like stars.
And Rio sleeps:
the sea is a dream
in which it dies and is reborn.

The bus speeds.
A violet cloud
unravels in its wake.
My legs begin to shake.

My lungs fill up with steam.
Sweat covers my face
and falls to my chest.
My neck and shoulders ache.

Not even sure
that I am awake,
I grip the hot
edge of the seat.

The driver smiles.
His pants are rolled above his knees
and his bare calves
gleam in the heat.

A woman tries to comfort me.
She puts her hand under my shirt
and writes the names of flowers
on my back.

Her skirt is black.
She has a tiny skull
and crossbones on each knee.
There is a garden in her eyes

where rows of dull,
white tombstones crowd the air
and people stand,
waving goodbye.

I have the feeling I am there.
She whispers through her teeth
and puts her lips
against my cheek.

The driver turns.
His eyes are closed and he is combing
back his hair.
He tells me to be brave.

I feel my heartbeat
growing fainter as he speaks.
The woman kisses me again.
Her jaw creaks

and her breath clings
to my neck like mist.
I turn to the window's
cracked pane

streaked with rain.
Where have I been?
I look toward Rio—
nothing is the same.

The Christ who stood
in a pool of electric light
high on his hill
is out of sight.

And the bay is black.
And the black city
sinks into its grave.
And I shall never come back.

WHAT TO THINK OF

Think of the jungle,
The green steam rising.

It is yours.
You are the prince of Paraguay.

Your minions kneel
Deep in the shade of giant leaves

While you drive by
Benevolent as gold.

They kiss the air
That moments before

Swept over your skin,
And rise only after you've passed.

Think of yourself, almost a god,
Your hair on fire,

The bellows of your heart pumping.
Think of the bats

Rushing out of their caves
Like a dark wind to greet you;

Of the vast nocturnal cities
Of lightning bugs

Floating down
From Minas Gerais;

Of the coral snakes;
Of the crimson birds

With emerald beaks;
Of the tons and tons of morpho butterflies

Filling the air
Like the cold confetti of paradise.

THE DIRTY HAND

My hand is dirty.
I must cut it off.
To wash it is pointless.
The water is putrid.
The soap is bad.
It won't lather.
The hand is dirty.
It's been dirty for years.

I used to keep it
out of sight,
in my pants pocket.
No one suspected a thing.
People came up to me,
wanting to shake hands.
I would refuse
and the hidden hand,
like a dark slug,
would leave its imprint
on my thigh.
And then I realized
it was the same
if I used it or not.
Disgust was the same.

Ah! How many nights
in the depths of the house
I washed that hand,
scrubbed it, polished it,
dreamed it would turn
to diamond or crystal
or even, at last,
into a plain white hand,
the clean hand of a man,
that you could shake,
or kiss, or hold
in one of those moments
when two people confess
without saying a word . . .
Only to have
the incurable hand,
lethargic and crablike,
open its dirty fingers.

(AFTER CARLOS DRUMMOND DE ANDRADE)

And the dirt was vile.
It was not mud or soot
or the caked filth
of an old scab
or the sweat
of a laborer's shirt.
It was a sad dirt
made of sickness
and human anguish.
It was not black;
black is pure.
It was dull,
a dull grayish dirt.

It is impossible
to live with this
gross hand that lies
on the table.
Quick! Cut it off!
Chop it to pieces
and throw it
into the ocean.
With time, with hope
and its intricate workings
another hand will come,
pure, transparent as glass,
and fasten itself to my arm.

THE TUNNEL

A man has been standing
in front of my house
for days. I peek at him
from the living room
window and at night,
unable to sleep,
I shine my flashlight
down on the lawn.
He is always there.

After a while
I open the front door
just a crack and order
him out of my yard.
He narrows his eyes
and moans. I slam
the door and dash back
to the kitchen, then up
to the bedroom, then down.

I weep like a schoolgirl
and make obscene gestures
through the window. I
write large suicide notes
and place them so he
can read them easily.
I destroy the living
room furniture to prove
I own nothing of value.

When he seems unmoved
I decide to dig a tunnel
to a neighboring yard.
I seal the basement off
from the upstairs with
a brick wall. I dig hard
and in no time the tunnel
is done. Leaving my pick
and shovel below,

I come out in front of a house
and stand there too tired to
move or even speak, hoping
someone will help me.
I feel I'm being watched
and sometimes I hear
a man's voice,
but nothing is done
and I have been waiting for days.

MOONTAN

for Donald Justice

The bluish, pale
face of the house
rises above me
like a wall of ice

and the distant,
solitary
barking of an owl
floats toward me.

I half close my eyes.
Over the damp
dark of the garden
flowers swing
back and forth
like small balloons.

The solemn trees,
each buried
in a cloud of leaves,
seem lost in sleep.

It is late.
I lie in the grass,
smoking,
feeling at ease,
pretending the end
will be like this.

Moonlight
falls on my flesh.
A breeze
circles my wrist.

I drift.
I shiver.
I know that soon
the day will come
to wash away the moon's
white stain,

that I shall walk
in the morning sun
invisible
as anyone.

THE DREAM

The top of my head opens
and out you go
into the pink and violet light of morning.

How bold you are!
You rise like the moon
while I sit on the edge of my bed,

afraid to move.
A breeze comes in the window,
brushes against my cheek, and I feel you shiver.

You will not last the day.
When they see you,
dogs will bark,

children will run to their mothers,
and birds will flock to you for shade.
You shrink at the thought.

Come back!
Bring the girls, the doctor, and the samba band!
There's plenty of room.

I shall close my eyes
and lie down in the dark
and look at you.

THE MAN IN BLACK

I was walking downtown
when I noticed a man in black,
black cape and black boots, coming toward me.

His arms out in front of him,
his fingers twinkling with little rings,
he looked like a summer night full of stars.

It was summer. The night was full of stars.
The tall buildings formed a hallway down which I walked.
The man in black came toward me.

The waxed tips of his mustache shone
like tiny spears and his teeth glistened.
I offered him my hand which he did not take.

I felt like a fool and stood in his black wake,
shaken and small, and my tears
swung back and forth in the sultry air like chandeliers.

VIOLENT STORM

Those who have chosen to pass the night
Entertaining friends
And intimate ideas in the bright,
Commodious rooms of dreams
Will not feel the slightest tremor
Or be wakened by what seems
Only a quirk in the dry run
Of conventional weather. For them,
The long night sweeping over these trees
And houses will have been no more than one
In a series whose end
Only the nervous or morbid consider.
But for us, the wide awake, who tend
To believe the worst is always waiting
Around the next corner or hiding in the dry,
Unsteady branch of a sick tree, debating
Whether or not to fell the passerby,
It has a sinister air.
How we wish we were sunning ourselves
In a world of familiar views
And fixed conditions, confined
By what we know, and able to refuse
Entry to the unaccounted for. For now,
Deeper and darker than ever, the night unveils
Its dubious plans, and the rain
Beats down in gales
Against the roof. We sit behind
Closed windows, bolted doors,
Unsure and ill at ease

While the loose, untidy wind,
Making an almost human sound, pours
Through the open chambers of the trees.
We cannot take ourselves or what belongs
To us for granted. No longer the exclusive,
Last resorts in which we could unwind,
Lounging in easy chairs,
Recalling the various wrongs
We had been done or spared, our rooms
Seem suddenly mixed up in our affairs.
We do not feel protected
By the walls, nor can we hide
Before the duplicating presence
Of their mirrors, pretending we are the ones who stare
From the other side, collected
In the glassy air.
A cold we never knew invades our bones.
We shake as though the storm were going to hurl us down
Against the flat stones
Of our lives. All other nights
Seem pale compared to this, and the brilliant rise
Of morning after morning seems unthinkable.
Already now the lights
That shared our wakefulness are dimming
And the dark brushes against our eyes.

THE SUICIDE

I jump from a building
As if I were falling asleep,

The wind like a pillow
Slowing me down,

Slowing me down
As if I were dreaming.

Surrounded by air,
I come to a stop,

And stand like a tourist
Watching the pigeons.

People in offices,
Wanting to save me,

Open their mouths.
"Throw me a stone," I yell,

Wanting to fall.
But nobody listens.

They throw me a rope.
And now I am walking,

Talking to you,
Talking to you

As if I were dreaming
I were alive.

KEEPING THINGS WHOLE

In a field
I am the absence
of field.
This is
always the case.
Wherever I am
I am what is missing.

When I walk
I part the air
and always
the air moves in
to fill the spaces
where my body's been.

We all have reasons
for moving.
I move
to keep things whole.

THE DOOR

The door is before you again and the shrieking
Starts and the mad voice is saying here here.
The myth of comfort dies and the couch of her
Body turns to dust. Clouds enter your eyes.

It is autumn. People are jumping from jetliners;
Their relatives leap into the air to join them.
That is what the shrieking is about. Nobody wants
To leave, nobody wants to stay behind.

The door is before you and you are unable to speak.
Your breathing is slow and you peer through
The window. Your doctor is wearing a butcher's apron
And carries a knife. You approve.

And you remember the first time you came. The leaves
Spun from the maples as you ran to the house.
You ran as you always imagined you would.
Your hand is on the door. This is where you came in.

THE DEAD

The graves grow deeper.
The dead are more dead each night.

Under the elms and the rain of leaves,
The graves grow deeper.

The dark folds of the wind
Cover the ground. The night is cold.

The leaves are swept against the stones.
The dead are more dead each night.

A starless dark embraces them.
Their faces dim.

We cannot remember them
Clearly enough. We never will.

THE MAN IN THE MIRROR

for Decio de Souza

I walk down the narrow,
carpeted hall.
The house is set.
The carnation in my buttonhole

precedes me like a small
continuous explosion.
The mirror
is in the living room.

You are there.
Your face is white, unsmiling, swollen.
The fallen body of your hair
is dull and out of place.

Buried in the darkness of your pockets,
your hands are motionless.
You do not seem awake.
Your skin sleeps

and your eyes lie in the deep
blue of their sockets,
impossible to reach.
How long will all this take?

I remember how we used to stand
wishing the glass
would dissolve between us,
and how we watched our words

cloud that bland,
innocent surface,
and when our faces blurred
how scared we were.

But that was another life.
One day you turned away
and left me here
to founder in the stillness of your wake.

Your suit floating, your hair
moving like eel grass
in a shallow bay, you drifted
out of the mirror's room, through the hall

and into the open air.
You seemed to rise and fall
with the wind, the sway
taking you always farther away, farther away.

Darkness filled your sleeves.
The stars moved through you.
The vague music of your shrieking
blossomed in my ears.

I tried forgetting what I saw;
I got down on the floor,
pretending to be dead.
It did not work.

My heart bunched in my rib cage like a bat,
blind and cowardly,
beating in and out,
a solemn, irreducible black.

The things you drove me to!
I walked in the calm of the house,
calling you back.
You did not answer.

I sat in a chair
and stared across the room.
The walls were bare.
The mirror was nothing without you.

I lay down on the couch
and closed my eyes.
My thoughts rose in the dark
like faint balloons,

and I would turn them over
one by one and watch them shiver.
I always fell into a deep
and arid sleep.

Then out of nowhere late one night
you reappeared,
a huge vegetable moon,
a bruise coated with light.

You stood before me,
dreamlike and obscene,
your face lost
under layers of heavy skin,

your body sunk in a green
and wrinkled sea of clothing.
I tried to help you
but you refused.

Days passed
and I would rest
my cheek against the glass,
wanting nothing but the old you.

I sang so sadly
that the neighbors wept
and dogs whined with pity.
Some things I wish I could forget.

You didn't care,
standing still while flies
collected in your hair
and dust fell like a screen before your eyes.

You never spoke
or tried to come up close.
Why did I want so badly
to get through to you?

It still goes on.
I go into the living room and you are there.
You drift in a pool
of silver air

where wounds and dreams of wounds
rise from the deep
humus of sleep
to bloom like flowers against the glass.

I look at you
and see myself
under the surface.
A dark and private weather

settles down on everything.
It is colder
and the dreams wither away.
You stand

like a shade
in the painless glass,
frail, distant, older
than ever.

It will always be this way.
I stand here scared
that you will disappear,
scared that you will stay.

DARKER

THE NEW POETRY HANDBOOK

for Greg Orr and Greg Simon

1   If a man understands a poem,
      he shall have troubles.

2   If a man lives with a poem,
      he shall die lonely.

3   If a man lives with two poems,
      he shall be unfaithful to one.

4   If a man conceives of a poem,
      he shall have one less child.

5   If a man conceives of two poems,
      he shall have two children less.

6   If a man wears a crown on his head as he writes,
      he shall be found out.

7   If a man wears no crown on his head as he writes,
      he shall deceive no one but himself.

8   If a man gets angry at a poem,
      he shall be scorned by men.

9   If a man continues to be angry at a poem,
      he shall be scorned by women.

10   If a man publicly denounces poetry,
      his shoes will fill with urine.

11   If a man gives up poetry for power,
      he shall have lots of power.

12   If a man brags about his poems,
      he shall be loved by fools.

13   If a man brags about his poems and loves fools,
      he shall write no more.

14 If a man denies his poems pleasure,
     his wit shall wear boots.

15 If a man craves attention because of his poems,
     he shall be like a jackass in moonlight.

16 If a man writes a poem and praises the poem of a fellow,
     he shall have a beautiful mistress.

17 If a man writes a poem and praises the poem of a fellow overly,
     he shall drive his mistress away.

18 If a man claims the poem of another,
     his heart shall double in size.

19 If a man lets his poems go naked,
     he shall fear death.

20 If a man fears death,
     he shall be saved by his poems.

21 If a man does not fear death,
     he may or may not be saved by his poems.

22 If a man finishes a poem,
     he shall bathe in the blank wake of his passion
     and be kissed by white paper.

BREATH

When you see them
tell them I am still here,
that I stand on one leg while the other one dreams,
that this is the only way,

that the lies I tell them are different
from the lies I tell myself,
that by being both here and beyond
I am becoming a horizon,

that as the sun rises and sets I know my place,
that breath is what saves me,
that even the forced syllables of decline are breath,
that if the body is a coffin it is also a closet of breath,

that breath is a mirror clouded by words,
that breath is all that survives the cry for help
as it enters the stranger's ear
and stays long after the word is gone,

that breath is the beginning again, that from it
all resistance falls away, as meaning falls
away from life, or darkness falls from light,
that breath is what I give them when I send my love.

LETTER

for Richard Howard

Men are running across a field,
pens fall from their pockets.
People out walking will pick them up.
It is one of the ways letters are written.

How things fall to others!
The self no longer belonging to me, but asleep
in a stranger's shadow, now clothing
the stranger, now leading him off.

It is noon as I write to you.
Someone's life has come into my hands.
The sun whitens the buildings.
It is all I have. I give it all to you. Yours,

GIVING MYSELF UP

I give up my eyes which are glass eggs.
I give up my tongue.
I give up my mouth which is the constant dream of my tongue.
I give up my throat which is the sleeve of my voice.
I give up my heart which is a burning apple.
I give up my lungs which are trees that have never seen the moon.
I give up my smell which is that of a stone traveling through rain.
I give up my hands which are ten wishes.
I give up my arms which have wanted to leave me anyway.
I give up my legs which are lovers only at night.
I give up my buttocks which are the moons of childhood.
I give up my penis which whispers encouragement to my thighs.
I give up my clothes which are walls that blow in the wind
and I give up the ghost that lives in them.
I give up. I give up.
And you will have none of it because already I am beginning
again without anything.

TOMORROW

Your best friend is gone,
your other friend, too.
Now the dream that used to turn in your sleep,
like a diamond, sails into the year's coldest night.

What did you say?
Or was it something you did?
It makes no difference—the house of breath collapsing
around your voice, your voice burning, are nothing to worry about.

Tomorrow your friends will come back;
your moist open mouth will bloom in the glass of storefronts.
Yes. Yes. Tomorrow they will come back and you
will invent an ending that comes out right.

THE ROOM

It is an old story, the way it happens
sometimes in winter, sometimes not.
The listener falls to sleep,
the doors to the closets of his unhappiness open

and into his room the misfortunes come—
death by daybreak, death by nightfall,
their wooden wings bruising the air,
their shadows the spilled milk the world cries over.

There is a need for surprise endings;
the green field where cows burn like newsprint,
where the farmer sits and stares,
where nothing, when it happens, is never terrible enough.

NOSTALGIA

for Donald Justice

The professors of English have taken their gowns
to the laundry, have taken themselves to the fields.
Dreams of motion circle the Persian rug in a room you were in.
On the beach the sadness of gramophones
deepens the ocean's folding and falling.
It is yesterday. It is still yesterday.

THE REMAINS

for Bill and Sandy Bailey

I empty myself of the names of others. I empty my pockets.
I empty my shoes and leave them beside the road.
At night I turn back the clocks;
I open the family album and look at myself as a boy.

What good does it do? The hours have done their job.
I say my own name. I say goodbye.
The words follow each other downwind.
I love my wife but send her away.

My parents rise out of their thrones
into the milky rooms of clouds. How can I sing?
Time tells me what I am. I change and I am the same.
I empty myself of my life and my life remains.

THE DANCE

The ghost of another comes to visit and we hold
communion while the light shines.
While the light shines, what else can we do?
And who doesn't have one foot in the grave?

I notice how the trees seem shaggy with leaves
and the steam of insects engulfs them.
The light falls like an anchor through the branches.
And which one of us is not being pulled down constantly?

My mind floats in the purple air of my skull.
I see myself dancing. I smile at everybody.
Slowly I dance out of the burning house of my head.
And who isn't borne again and again into heaven?

THE GOOD LIFE

You stand at the window.
There is a glass cloud in the shape of a heart.
There are the wind's sighs that are like caves in your speech.
You are the ghost in the tree outside.

The street is quiet.
The weather, like tomorrow, like your life,
is partially here, partially up in the air.
There is nothing you can do.

The good life gives no warning.
It weathers the climates of despair
and appears, on foot, unrecognized, offering nothing,
and you are there.

THE DRESS

Lie down on the bright hill
with the moon's hand on your cheek,
your flesh deep in the white folds of your dress,
and you will not hear the passionate mole
extending the length of his darkness,
or the owl arranging all of the night,
which is his wisdom, or the poem
filling your pillow with its blue feathers.
But if you step out of your dress and move into the shade,
the mole will find you, so will the owl, and so will the poem,
and you will fall into another darkness, one you will find
yourself making and remaking until it is perfect.

THE GUARDIAN

The sun setting. The lawns on fire.
The lost day, the lost light.
Why do I love what fades?

You who left, who were leaving,
what dark rooms do you inhabit?
Guardian of my death,

preserve my absence. I am alive.

THE HILL

I have come this far on my own legs,
missing the bus, missing taxis,
climbing always. One foot in front of the other,
that is the way I do it.

It does not bother me, the way the hill goes on.
Grass beside the road, a tree rattling
its black leaves. So what?
The longer I walk, the farther I am from everything.

One foot in front of the other. The hours pass.
One foot in front of the other. The years pass.
The colors of arrival fade.
That is the way I do it.

COMING TO THIS

We have done what we wanted.
We have discarded dreams, preferring the heavy industry
of each other, and we have welcomed grief
and called ruin the impossible habit to break.

And now we are here.
The dinner is ready and we cannot eat.
The meat sits in the white lake of its dish.
The wine waits.

Coming to this
has its rewards: nothing is promised, nothing is taken away.
We have no heart or saving grace,
no place to go, no reason to remain.

II   *Black Maps*

THE SLEEP

There is the sleep of my tongue
speaking a language I can never remember—
words that enter the sleep of words
once they are spoken.

There is the sleep of one moment
inside the next, lengthening the night,
and the sleep of the window
turning the tall sleep of trees into glass.

The sleep of novels as they are read is soundless
like the sleep of dresses on the warm bodies of women.
And the sleep of thunder gathering dust on sunny days
and the sleep of ashes long after.

The sleep of wind has been known to fill the sky.
The long sleep of air locked in the lungs of the dead.
The sleep of a room with someone inside it.
Even the wooden sleep of the moon is possible.

And there is the sleep that demands I lie down
and be fitted to the dark that comes upon me
like another skin in which I shall never be found,
out of which I shall never appear.

BLACK MAPS

Not the attendance of stones,
nor the applauding wind,
shall let you know
you have arrived,

nor the sea that celebrates
only departures,
nor the mountains,
nor the dying cities.

Nothing will tell you
where you are.
Each moment is a place
you've never been.

You can walk
believing you cast
a light around you.
But how will you know?

The present is always dark.
Its maps are black,
rising from nothing,
describing,

in their slow ascent
into themselves,
their own voyage,
its emptiness,

the bleak, temperate
necessity of its completion.
As they rise into being
they are like breath.

And if they are studied at all
it is only to find,
too late, what you thought
were concerns of yours

do not exist.
Your house is not marked
on any of them,
nor are your friends,

waiting for you to appear,
nor are your enemies,
listing your faults.
Only you are there,

saying hello
to what you will be,
and the black grass
is holding up the black stars.

SEVEN POEMS

1

At the edge
of the body's night
ten moons are rising.

2

A scar remembers the wound.
The wound remembers the pain.
Once more you are crying.

3

When we walk in the sun
our shadows are like barges of silence.

4

My body lies down
and I hear my own
voice lying next to me.

5

The rock is pleasure
and it opens
and we enter it
as we enter ourselves
each night.

6

When I talk to the window
I say everything
is everything.

7

I have a key
so I open the door and walk in.
It is dark and I walk in.
It is darker and I walk in.

FROM A LITANY

There in an open field I lie down in a hole I once dug and I
    praise the sky.

I praise the clouds that are like lungs of light.

I praise the owl that wants to inhabit me and the hawk that
    does not.

I praise the mouse's fury, the wolf's consideration.

I praise the dog that lives in the household of people and
    shall never be one of them.

I praise the whale that lives under the cold blankets of salt.

I praise the formations of squid, the domes of meandra.

I praise the secrecy of doors, the openness of windows.

I praise the depth of closets.

I praise the wind, the rising generations of air.

I praise the trees on whose branches shall sit the Cock of
    Portugal and the Polish Cock.

I praise the palm trees of Rio and those that shall grow in
    London.

I praise the gardeners, the worms and the small plants that
    praise each other.

I praise the sweet berries of Georgetown, Maine and the
    song of the white-throated sparrow.

I praise the poets of Waverly Place and Eleventh Street, and
    the one whose bones turn to dark emeralds when he
    stands upright in the wind.

I praise the clocks for which I grow old in a day and young
    in a day.

I praise all manner of shade, that which I see and that which
    I do not.

I praise all roofs from the watery roof of the pond to the
  slate roof of the customs house.
I praise those who have made of their bodies final embassies
  of flesh.
I praise the failure of those with ambition, the authors of
  leaflets and notebooks of nothing.
I praise the moon for suffering men.
I praise the sun its tributes.
I praise the pain of revival and the bliss of decline.
I praise all for nothing because there is no price.
I praise myself for the way I have with a shovel and I praise
  the shovel.
I praise the motive of praise by which I shall be reborn.
I praise the morning whose sun is upon me.
I praise the evening whose son I am.

THE RECOVERY

I stood alone in the weather
and wished I were wrapped in the stones,
the long sheets, the bones of my father
laid out in the ground, and later,

after waiting, and watching
the sun fall into the hills and the night
close down over the least light,
I walked to the water's edge

and saw the doctors wave from the deck of a boat
that steamed from port, their bags open,
their instruments shining like ruins under the moon,
and it was no more than anyone might have predicted.

THE PREDICTION

That night the moon drifted over the pond,
turning the water to milk, and under
the boughs of the trees, the blue trees,
a young woman walked, and for an instant

the future came to her:
rain falling on her husband's grave, rain falling
on the lawns of her children, her own mouth
filling with cold air, strangers moving into her house,

a man in her room writing a poem, the moon drifting into it,
a woman strolling under its trees, thinking of death,
thinking of him thinking of her, and the wind rising
and taking the moon and leaving the paper dark.

THE ONE SONG

I prefer to sit all day
like a sack in a chair
and to lie all night
like a stone in my bed.

When food comes
I open my mouth.
When sleep comes
I close my eyes.

My body sings
only one song;
the wind turns
gray in my arms.

Flowers bloom.
Flowers die.
More is less.
I long for more.

THE STONE

The stone lives on.
The followers of the man with the glass face
walk around it
with their glass legs
and glass arms.

The stone lives on.
It lives on air.
It lives on your looking.
It lives inside and outside
itself and is never clear
which is which.

That is why
the followers of the man with the glass face
walk around it proposing
the possibilities
of emptiness.

The stone lives on,
commending itself to the hardness of air,
to the long meadows of your looking.

FROM A LITANY

Let the shark keep to the shelves and closets of coral.
Let cats throw over their wisdom.
Let the noble horse who rocks under the outlaw's ass eat plastic turf.
For no creature is safe.
Let the great sow of state grow strong.
Let those in office search under their clothes for the private life.
They will find nothing.
Let them gather together and hold hands.
They shall have nothing to hold.
Let the flag flutter in the glass moon of each eye.
Let the black-suited priests stand for the good life.
Let them tell us to be more like them.
For that is the nature of the sickness.
Let the bodies of debutantes gleam like frigidaires.
For they shall have sex with food.
Let flies sink into their mothers' thighs and go blind in the
    trenches of meat.
Let the patient unmask the doctor and swim in the gray milk of
    his mind.
For nothing will keep.
Let the bleak faces of the police swell like yeast.
Let breezes run like sauce over their skins.
For this kingdom is theirs.
Let a violet cloak fall on the bleached hair of the poetess.
Let twilight cover the lost bone of her passion.
For her moon is ambition.
Let the dusty air release its sugars.
Let candy the color of marlin flesh build up on the tables.
For everyone's mouth is open.
Let the wind devise secrets and leave them in trees.
Let the earth suck at roots and discover the emblems of weather.

III *My Life by Somebody Else*

MY LIFE

The huge doll of my body
refuses to rise.
I am the toy of women.
My mother

would prop me up for her friends.
"Talk, talk," she would beg.
I moved my mouth
but words did not come.

My wife took me down from the shelf.
I lay in her arms. "We suffer
the sickness of self," she would whisper.
And I lay there dumb.

Now my daughter
gives me a plastic nurser
filled with water.
"You are my real baby," she says.

Poor child!
I look into the brown
mirrors of her eyes
and see myself

diminishing, sinking down
to a depth she does not know is there.
Out of breath,
I will not rise again.

I grow into my death.
My life is small
and getting smaller. The world is green.
Nothing is all.

MY DEATH

Sadness, of course, and confusion.
The relatives gathered at the graveside,
talking about the waste, and the weather mounting,
the rain moving in vague pillars offshore.

This is Prince Edward Island.
I came back to my birthplace to announce my death.
I said I would ride full gallop into the sea
and not look back. People were furious.

I told them about attempts I had made in the past,
how I starved in order to be the size of Lucille,
whom I loved, to inhabit the cold space
her body had taken. They were shocked.

I went on about the time
I dove in a perfect arc that filled
with the sunshine of farewell and I fell
head over shoulders into the river's thigh.

And about the time
I stood naked in the snow, pointing a pistol
between my eyes, and how when I fired my head bloomed
into health. Soon I was alone.

Now I lie in the box
of my making while the weather
builds and the mourners shake their heads as if
to write or to die, I did not have to do either.

MY LIFE BY SOMEBODY ELSE

I have done what I could but you avoid me.
I left a bowl of milk on the desk to tempt you.
Nothing happened. I left my wallet there, full of money.
You must have hated me for that. You never came.

I sat at my typewriter naked, hoping you would wrestle me
to the floor. I played with myself just to arouse you.
Boredom drove me to sleep. I offered you my wife.
I sat her on the desk and spread her legs. I waited.

The days drag on. The exhausted light falls like a bandage
over my eyes. Is it because I am ugly? Was anyone
ever so sad? It is pointless to slash my wrists. My hands
would fall off. And then what hope would I have?

Why do you never come? Must I have you by being
somebody else? Must I write *My Life* by somebody else?
My Death by somebody else? Are you listening?
Somebody else has arrived. Somebody else is writing.

COURTSHIP

There is a girl you like so you tell her
your penis is big, but that you cannot get yourself
to use it. Its demands are ridiculous, you say,
even self-defeating, but to be honored somehow,
briefly, inconspicuously in the dark.

When she closes her eyes in horror,
you take it all back. You tell her you're almost
a girl yourself and can understand why she is shocked.
When she is about to walk away, you tell her
you have no penis, that you don't

know what got into you. You get on your knees.
She suddenly bends down to kiss your shoulder and you know
you're on the right track. You tell her you want
to bear children and that is why you seem confused.
You wrinkle your brow and curse the day you were born.

She tries to calm you, but you lose control.
You reach for her panties and beg forgiveness as you do.
She squirms and you howl like a wolf. Your craving
seems monumental. You know you will have her.
Taken by storm, she is the girl you will marry.

ELEGY 1969

You slave away into your old age
and nothing you do adds up to much.
Day after day you go through the same motions,
you shiver in bed, you get hungry, you want a woman.

Heroes standing for lives of sacrifice and obedience
fill the parks through which you walk.
At night in the fog they open their bronze umbrellas
or else withdraw to the empty lobbies of movie houses.

You love the night for its power of annihilating,
but while you sleep, your problems will not let you die.
Waking only proves the existence of The Great Machine
and the hard light falls on your shoulders.

You walk among the dead and talk
about times to come and matters of the spirit.
Literature wasted your best hours of lovemaking.
Weekends were lost, cleaning your apartment.

You are quick to confess your failure and to postpone
collective joy to the next century. You accept
rain, war, unemployment and the unjust distribution of wealth
because you can't, all by yourself, blow up Manhattan Island.

(AFTER CARLOS DRUMMOND DE ANDRADE)

"THE DREADFUL HAS ALREADY HAPPENED"

The relatives are leaning over, staring expectantly.
They moisten their lips with their tongues. I can feel
them urging me on. I hold the baby in the air.
Heaps of broken bottles glitter in the sun.

A small band is playing old fashioned marches.
My mother is keeping time by stamping her foot.
My father is kissing a woman who keeps waving
to somebody else. There are palm trees.

The hills are spotted with orange flamboyants and tall
billowy clouds move behind them. "Go on, boy,"
I hear somebody say, "Go on."
I keep wondering if it will rain.

The sky darkens. There is thunder.
"Break his legs," says one of my aunts,
"now give him a kiss." I do what I'm told.
The trees bend in the bleak tropical wind.

The baby did not scream, but I remember that sigh
when I reached inside for his tiny lungs and shook them
out in the air for the flies. The relatives cheered.
It was about that time I gave up.

Now, when I answer the phone, his lips
are in the receiver; when I sleep, his hair is gathered
around a familiar face on the pillow; wherever I search
I find his feet. He is what is left of my life.

NOT DYING

These wrinkles are nothing.
These gray hairs are nothing.
This stomach which sags
with old food, these bruised
and swollen ankles,
my darkening brain,
they are nothing.
I am the same boy
my mother used to kiss.

The years change nothing.
On windless summer nights
I feel those kisses
slide from her dark
lips far away,
and in winter they float
over the frozen pines
and arrive covered with snow.
They keep me young.

My passion for milk
is uncontrollable still.
I am driven by innocence.
From bed to chair I crawl
and back again.
I shall not die.
The grave result
and token of birth, my body
remembers and holds fast.

THE WAY IT IS

The world is ugly
And the people are sad.
—WALLACE STEVENS

I lie in bed.
I toss all night
in the cold unruffled deep
of my sheets and cannot sleep.

My neighbor marches in his room,
wearing the sleek
mask of a hawk with a large beak.
He stands by the window. A violet plume

rises from his helmet's dome.
The moon's light
spills over him like milk and the wind rinses the white
glass bowls of his eyes.

His helmet in a shopping bag,
he sits in the park, waving a small American flag.
He cannot be heard as he moves
behind trees and hedges,

always at the frayed edges
of town, pulling a gun on someone like me. I crouch
under the kitchen table, telling myself
I am a dog, who would kill a dog?

My neighbor's wife comes home.
She walks into the living room,
takes off her clothes, her hair falls down her back.
She seems to wade

through long flat rivers of shade.
The soles of her feet are black.
She kisses her husband's neck
and puts her hands inside his pants.

My neighbors dance.
They roll on the floor, his tongue
is in her ear, his lungs
reek with the swill and weather of hell.

Out on the street people are lying down
with their knees in the air, tears
fill their eyes, ashes
cover their ears.

Their clothes are torn
from their backs. Their faces are worn.
Horsemen are riding around them, telling them why
they should die.

My neighbor's wife calls to me, her mouth is pressed
against the wall behind my bed.
She says, "My husband's dead."
I turn over on my side,

hoping she has not lied.
The walls and ceiling of my room are gray—
the moon's color through the windows of a laundromat.
I close my eyes.

I see myself float
on the dead sea of my bed, falling away,
calling for help, but the vague scream
sticks in my throat.

I see myself in the park
on horseback, surrounded by dark,
leading the armies of peace.
The iron legs of the horse do not bend.

I drop the reins. Where will the turmoil end?
Fleets of taxis stall
in the fog, passengers fall
asleep. Gas pours

from a tricolored stack.
Locking their doors,
people from offices huddle together,
telling the same story over and over.

Everyone who has sold himself wants to buy himself back.
Nothing is done. The night
eats into their limbs
like a blight.

Everything dims.
The future is not what it used to be.
The graves are ready. The dead
shall inherit the dead.

THE STORY OF OUR LIVES

ELEGY FOR MY FATHER

(Robert Strand, 1908–68)

1 THE EMPTY BODY

The hands were yours, the arms were yours,
But you were not there.
The eyes were yours, but they were closed and would not open.
The distant sun was there.
The moon poised on the hill's white shoulder was there.
The wind on Bedford Basin was there.
The pale green light of winter was there.
Your mouth was there,
But you were not there.
When somebody spoke, there was no answer.
Clouds came down
And buried the buildings along the water,
And the water was silent.
The gulls stared.
The years, the hours, that would not find you
Turned in the wrists of others.
There was no pain. It had gone.
There were no secrets. There was nothing to say.
The shade scattered its ashes.
The body was yours, but you were not there.
The air shivered against its skin.
The dark leaned into its eyes.
But you were not there.

2 ANSWERS

Why did you travel?
Because the house was cold.
Why did you travel?
Because it is what I have always done between sunset and sunrise.
What did you wear?
I wore a blue suit, a white shirt, yellow tie, and yellow socks.
What did you wear?
I wore nothing. A scarf of pain kept me warm.
Who did you sleep with?
I slept with a different woman each night.
Who did you sleep with?
I slept alone. I have always slept alone.
Why did you lie to me?
I always thought I told the truth.
Why did you lie to me?
Because the truth lies like nothing else and I love the truth.
Why are you going?
Because nothing means much to me anymore.
Why are you going?
I don't know. I have never known.
How long shall I wait for you?
Do not wait for me. I am tired and I want to lie down.
Are you tired and do you want to lie down?
Yes, I am tired and I want to lie down.

3 YOUR DYING

Nothing could stop you.
Not the best day. Not the quiet. Not the ocean rocking.
You went on with your dying.
Not the trees

Under which you walked, not the trees that shaded you.
Not the doctor
Who warned you, the white-haired young doctor who saved you once.
You went on with your dying.
Nothing could stop you. Not your son. Not your daughter
Who fed you and made you into a child again.
Not your son who thought you would live forever.
Not the wind that shook your lapels.
Not the stillness that offered itself to your motion.
Not your shoes that grew heavier.
Not your eyes that refused to look ahead.
Nothing could stop you.
You sat in your room and stared at the city
And went on with your dying.
You went to work and let the cold enter your clothes.
You let blood seep into your socks.
Your face turned white.
Your voice cracked in two.
You leaned on your cane.
But nothing could stop you.
Not your friends who gave you advice.
Not your son. Not your daughter who watched you grow small.
Not fatigue that lived in your sighs.
Not your lungs that would fill with water.
Not your sleeves that carried the pain of your arms.
Nothing could stop you.
You went on with your dying.
When you played with children you went on with your dying.
When you sat down to eat,
When you woke up at night, wet with tears, your body sobbing,
You went on with your dying.
Nothing could stop you.
Not the past.

Not the future with its good weather.
Not the view from your window, the view of the graveyard.
Not the city. Not the terrible city with its wooden buildings.
Not defeat. Not success.
You did nothing but go on with your dying.
You put your watch to your ear.
You felt yourself slipping.
You lay on the bed.
You folded your arms over your chest and you dreamed of the
    world without you,
Of the space under the trees,
Of the space in your room,
Of the spaces that would now be empty of you,
And you went on with your dying.
Nothing could stop you.
Not your breathing. Not your life.
Not the life you wanted.
Not the life you had.
Nothing could stop you.

4 YOUR SHADOW

You have your shadow.
The places where you were have given it back.
The hallways and bare lawns of the orphanage have given it back.
The Newsboys' Home has given it back.
The streets of New York have given it back and so have the streets
    of Montreal.
The rooms in Belém where lizards would snap at mosquitos have
    given it back.
The dark streets of Manaus and the damp streets of Rio have given
    it back.
Mexico City where you wanted to leave it has given it back.

And Halifax where the harbor would wash its hands of you has
   given it back.
You have your shadow.
When you traveled the white wake of your going sent your shadow
   below, but when you arrived it was there to greet you. You had
   your shadow.
The doorways you entered lifted your shadow from you and when
   you went out, gave it back. You had your shadow.
Even when you forgot your shadow, you found it again; it had been
   with you.
Once in the country the shade of a tree covered your shadow and
   you were not known.
Once in the country you thought your shadow had been cast by
   somebody else. Your shadow said nothing.
Your clothes carried your shadow inside; when you took them off, it
   spread like the dark of your past.
And your words that float like leaves in an air that is lost, in a place
   no one knows, gave you back your shadow.
Your friends gave you back your shadow.
Your enemies gave you back your shadow. They said it was heavy
   and would cover your grave.
When you died your shadow slept at the mouth of the furnace and
   ate ashes for bread.
It rejoiced among ruins.
It watched while others slept.
It shone like crystal among the tombs.
It composed itself like air.
It wanted to be like snow on water.
It wanted to be nothing, but that was not possible.
It came to my house.
It sat on my shoulders.
Your shadow is yours. I told it so. I said it was yours.
I have carried it with me too long. I give it back.

5 MOURNING

They mourn for you.
When you rise at midnight,
And the dew glitters on the stone of your cheeks,
They mourn for you.
They lead you back into the empty house.
They carry the chairs and tables inside.
They sit you down and teach you to breathe.
And your breath burns,
It burns the pine box and the ashes fall like sunlight.
They give you a book and tell you to read.
They listen and their eyes fill with tears.
The women stroke your fingers.
They comb the yellow back into your hair.
They shave the frost from your beard.
They knead your thighs.
They dress you in fine clothes.
They rub your hands to keep them warm.
They feed you. They offer you money.
They get on their knees and beg you not to die.
When you rise at midnight they mourn for you.
They close their eyes and whisper your name over and over.
But they cannot drag the buried light from your veins.
They cannot reach your dreams.
Old man, there is no way.
Rise and keep rising, it does no good.
They mourn for you the way they can.

6 THE NEW YEAR

It is winter and the new year.
Nobody knows you.

Away from the stars, from the rain of light,
You lie under the weather of stones.
There is no thread to lead you back.
Your friends doze in the dark
Of pleasure and cannot remember.
Nobody knows you. You are the neighbor of nothing.
You do not see the rain falling and the man walking away,
The soiled wind blowing its ashes across the city.
You do not see the sun dragging the moon like an echo.
You do not see the bruised heart go up in flames,
The skulls of the innocent turn into smoke.
You do not see the scars of plenty, the eyes without light.
It is over. It is winter and the new year.
The meek are hauling their skins into heaven.
The hopeless are suffering the cold with those who have nothing to
    hide.
It is over and nobody knows you.
There is starlight drifting on the black water.
There are stones in the sea no one has seen.
There is a shore and people are waiting.
And nothing comes back.
Because it is over.
Because there is silence instead of a name.
Because it is winter and the new year.

II *The Room*

THE ROOM

I stand at the back of a room
and you have just entered.
I feel the dust
fall from the air
onto my cheeks.
I feel the ice
of sunlight on the walls.
The trees outside
remind me of something
you are not yet aware of.
You have just entered.
There is something like sorrow
in the room.
I believe you think
it has wings
and will change me.
The room is so large
I wonder what you are thinking
or why you have come.
I ask you,
What are you doing?
You have just entered
and cannot hear me.
Where did you buy
the black coat you are wearing?
You told me once.
I cannot remember
what happened between us.
I am here. Can you see me?
I shall lay my words on the table

as if they were gloves,
as if nothing had happened.
I hear the wind
and I wonder what are
the blessings
born of enclosure.
The need to get away?
The desire to arrive?
I am so far away
I seem to be in the room's past
and so much here in
the room is beginning
to vanish around me.
It will be yours soon.
You have just entered.
I feel myself drifting,
beginning to be
somewhere else.
Houses are rising
out of my past,
people are walking
under the trees.
You do not see them.
You have just entered.
The room is long.
There is a table in the middle.
You will walk
toward the table,
toward the flowers,
toward the presence of sorrow
which has begun to move
among objects,
its wings beating

to the sound of your heart.
You shall come closer
and I shall begin to turn away.
The black coat you are wearing,
where did you get it?
You told me once
and I cannot remember.
I stand at the back
of the room and I know
if you close your eyes
you will know why
you are here;
that to stand in a space
is to forget time,
that to forget time
is to forget death.
Soon you will take off your coat.
Soon the room's whiteness
will be a skin for your body.
I feel the turning of breath
around what we are going to say.
I know by the way
you raise your hand
you have noticed the flowers
on the table.
They will lie
in the wake of our motions
and the room's map
will lie before us
like a simple rug.
You have just entered.
There is nothing to be done.
I stand at the back of the room

and I believe you see me.
The light consumes the chair,
absorbing its vacancy,
and will swallow itself
and release the darkness
that will fill the chair again.
I shall be gone.
You will say you are here.
I can hear you say it.
I can almost hear you say it.
Soon you will take off your black coat
and the room's whiteness
will close around you
and you will move
to the back of the room.
Your name will no longer be known,
nor will mine.
I stand at the back
and you have just entered.
The beginning is about to occur.
The end is in sight.

SHE

for Bill and Sandy Bailey

She slept without the usual concerns,
the troubling dreams—the pets
moving through the museum,
the carved monsters, the candles
giving themselves up to darkness.
She slept without caring what she looked like,
without considering the woman
who would come or the men who would leave
or the mirrors or the basin of cold water.
She slept on one side, the sheets
pouring into the room's cold air,
the pillow shapeless, her flesh
no longer familiar. Her sleep
was a form of neglect.
She did nothing for days,
the sun and moon had washed up
on the same shore. Her negligee
became her flesh, her flesh became
the soft folding of air over the sheets.
And there was no night, nor any sign of it.
Nothing curled in the air
but the sound of nothing,
the hymn of nothing, the humming
of the room, of its past.
Her flesh turned from itself
into the sheets of light.
She began to wake; her hair spilled
into the rivers of shadow.
Her eyes half-open, she saw the man across the room,
she watched him and could not choose

between sleep and wakefulness.
And he watched her
and the moment became their lives
so that she would never rise or turn from him,
so that he would always be there.

IN CELEBRATION

You sit in a chair, touched by nothing, feeling
the old self become the older self, imagining
only the patience of water, the boredom of stone.
You think that silence is the extra page,
you think that nothing is good or bad, not even
the darkness that fills the house while you sit watching
it happen. You've seen it happen before. Your friends
move past the window, their faces soiled with regret.
You want to wave but cannot raise your hand.
You sit in a chair. You turn to the nightshade spreading
a poisonous net around the house. You taste
the honey of absence. It is the same wherever
you are, the same if the voice rots before
the body, or the body rots before the voice.
You know that desire leads only to sorrow, that sorrow
leads to achievement which leads to emptiness.
You know that this is different, that this
is the celebration, the only celebration,
that by giving yourself over to nothing,
you shall be healed. You know there is joy in feeling
your lungs prepare themselves for an ashen future,
so you wait, you stare and you wait, and the dust settles
and the miraculous hours of childhood wander in darkness.

TO BEGIN

He lay in bed not knowing how to begin.
His mind was unclear, and whatever he felt
faded into an aspect of something
he had known already. Maybe
someone could tell him what to do.
Maybe he could say what he wanted
in his own voice and still be surprised,
say, for example, that it was just before dawn,
that the moon was still a prisoner to stone,
that the sun called so faintly
only a few birds heard it
and they sang for the light
the way some men sing for bread.
If he could say it so that people
believed him, so that he believed it,
he would go on. He would begin
to believe that waking meant
casting his sleep back into the night.
Later, he could learn to say what he meant
without actually saying it.
But he lay in bed, powerless to begin.

He thought how he had always carried
darkness into day where it blazed
into a likeness of himself.
He had stood like a ghost in sunlight,
barely visible, in whose eyes
the trees, the windows, the vanishings
of a previous life became real again.
Maybe he could say that.

But to whom? And for what reason?
To whom could he say that to lose
again and again is to have more
and more to lose, that losing is having?

There was no reason to get up.
Let the sun shine without him.
He knew he was not needed,
that his speech was a mirror, at best,
that once he had imagined his words
floating upward, luminous and threatening,
moving among the stars, becoming the stars,
becoming in the end the equal of all the dead
and the living. He had imagined this
and did not care to again.
If only he could say something,
something that had the precision
of his staying in bed.
It took no courage, no special
recklessness to discredit silence.
He had tried to do it, but had failed.
He had gone to bed and slept.
The phrases had disappeared, sinking
into sleep, unwanted and uncalled for.

He stared at the ceiling
and imagined his breath shaping itself into words.
He imagined that he would go to the water and look down,
that he would see the shimmer of fish
over the ruinous coral
and watch them die in the shade of his image.
But he could never say that.

Maybe the world would lighten
and without thinking he would be able to lift
from his back the wings of night
and lift the stones from his teeth
and would be able to speak.
But he could not say that either.
He could do nothing but lie there
and wait for the sun to go down,
wait for the promise of stillness
that would be sent from his heart into the field,
and wait for it to return.
And later he would lie there
and pretend it was morning.
In the dark he would still be uncertain of how to begin.
He would mumble to himself; he would follow
his words to learn where he was.
He would begin.
And the room, the house, the field,
the woods beyond the field, would also begin,
and in the sound of his own voice beginning
he would hear them.

III   *The Story of Our Lives*

THE STORY OF OUR LIVES

for Howard Moss

1

We are reading the story of our lives
which takes place in a room.
The room looks out on a street.
There is no one there,
no sound of anything.
The trees are heavy with leaves,
the parked cars never move.
We keep turning the pages,
hoping for something,
something like mercy or change,
a black line that would bind us
or keep us apart.
The way it is, it would seem
the book of our lives is empty.
The furniture in the room is never shifted,
and the rugs become darker each time
our shadows pass over them.
It is almost as if the room were the world.
We sit beside each other on the couch,
reading about the couch.
We say it is ideal.
It is ideal.

2

We are reading the story of our lives
as though we were in it,

as though we had written it.
This comes up again and again.
In one of the chapters
I lean back and push the book aside
because the book says
it is what I am doing.
I lean back and begin to write about the book.
I write that I wish to move beyond the book,
beyond my life into another life.
I put the pen down.
The book says: *He put the pen down*
and turned and watched her reading
the part about herself falling in love.
The book is more accurate than we can imagine.
I lean back and watch you read
about the man across the street.
They built a house there,
and one day a man walked out of it.
You fell in love with him
because you knew he would never visit you,
would never know you were waiting.
Night after night you would say
that he was like me.
I lean back and watch you grow older without me.
Sunlight falls on your silver hair.
The rugs, the furniture,
seem almost imaginary now.
She continued to read.
She seemed to consider his absence
of no special importance,
as someone on a perfect day will consider
the weather a failure
because it did not change his mind.

You narrow your eyes.
You have the impulse to close the book
which describes my resistance:
how when I lean back I imagine
my life without you, imagine moving
into another life, another book.
It describes your dependence on desire,
how the momentary disclosures
of purpose make you afraid.
The book describes much more than it should.
It wants to divide us.

3

This morning I woke and believed
there was no more to our lives
than the story of our lives.
When you disagreed, I pointed
to the place in the book where you disagreed.
You fell back to sleep and I began to read
those mysterious parts you used to guess at
while they were being written
and lose interest in after they became
part of the story.
In one of them cold dresses of moonlight
are draped over the backs of chairs in a man's room.
He dreams of a woman whose dresses are lost,
who sits on a stone bench in a garden
and believes in wonders.
For her love is a sacrifice.
The part describes her death
and she is never named,
which is one of the things

you could not stand about her.
A little later we learn
that the dreaming man lives
in the new house across the street.
This morning after you fell back to sleep
I began to turn pages early in the book:
it was like dreaming of childhood,
so much seemed to vanish,
so much seemed to come to life again.
I did not know what to do.
The book said: *In those moments it was his book.*
A bleak crown rested uneasily on his head.
He was the brief ruler of inner and outer discord,
anxious in his own kingdom.

4

Before you woke
I read another part that described your absence
and told how you sleep to reverse
the progress of your life.
I was touched by my own loneliness as I read,
knowing that what I feel is often the crude
and unsuccessful form of a story
that may never be told.
I read and was moved by a desire to offer myself
to the house of your sleep.
He wanted to see her naked and vulnerable,
to see her in the refuse, the discarded
plots of old dreams, the costumes and masks
of unattainable states.
It was as if he were drawn
irresistibly to failure.

It was hard to keep reading.
I was tired and wanted to give up.
The book seemed aware of this.
It hinted at changing the subject.
I waited for you to wake not knowing
how long I waited,
and it seemed that I was no longer reading.
I heard the wind passing
like a stream of sighs
and I heard the shiver of leaves
in the trees outside the window.
It would be in the book.
Everything would be there.
I looked at your face
and I read the eyes, the nose, the mouth . . .

5

If only there were a perfect moment in the book;
if only we could live in that moment,
we could begin the book again
as if we had not written it,
as if we were not in it.
But the dark approaches
to any page are too numerous
and the escapes are too narrow.
We read through the day.
Each page turning is like a candle
moving through the mind.
Each moment is like a hopeless cause.
If only we could stop reading.
He never wanted to read another book
and she kept staring into the street.

The cars were still there,
the deep shade of trees covered them.
The shades were drawn in the new house.
Maybe the man who lived there,
the man she loved, was reading
the story of another life.
She imagined a dank, heartless parlor,
a cold fireplace, a man sitting
writing a letter to a woman
who has sacrificed her life for love.
If there were a perfect moment in the book,
it would be the last.
The book never discusses the causes of love.
It claims confusion is a necessary good.
It never explains. It only reveals.

6

The day goes on.
We study what we remember.
We look into the mirror across the room.
We cannot bear to be alone.
The book goes on.
They became silent and did not know how to begin
the dialogue which was necessary.
It was words that created divisions in the first place,
that created loneliness.
They waited.
They would turn the pages, hoping
something would happen.
They would patch up their lives in secret:
each defeat forgiven because it could not be tested,

each pain rewarded because it was unreal.
They did nothing.

7

The book will not survive.
We are the living proof of that.
It is dark outside, in the room it is darker.
I hear your breathing.
You are asking me if I am tired,
if I want to keep reading.
Yes, I am tired.
Yes, I want to keep reading.
I say yes to everything.
You cannot hear me.
They sat beside each other on the couch.
They were the copy, the tired phantoms
of something they had been before.
The attitudes they took were jaded.
They stared into the book
and were horrified by their innocence,
their reluctance to give up.
They sat beside each other on the couch.
They were determined to accept the truth.
Whatever it was they would accept it.
The book would have to be written
and would have to be read.
They are the book and they are
nothing else.

INSIDE THE STORY

1

He never spoke much
but he began to speak even less.
And the chair in the living room was unsafe.
And the bed in the bedroom was never made.
And nothing was the same as it had been.
Still, he said he was happy.
He would look at the stars
and their distance confirmed what he felt.
If there was order, then he was a part of it;
if there was chaos, then it wasn't his fault.
He had no cause for anger.
When he spoke to his wife
the subject was always the same:
she would travel and see the world,
he would stay home and water the plants;
or, he would see the world and she
would water the plants.
Their lives continued.
She undressed in the dark bathroom.
He read a dull book in the kitchen.
Nothing changed until she admitted she loved him;
that night he slept in the living room,
alone, and had a dream.

2

He dreamed that he had gone,
and no one had seen him off.
Under the simple moon
the stones and bushes looked alike.
It was the end of summer and he could smell the grass
and feel the wind from the lake.
He loved farewells. He loved
not knowing where he was going,
and the dark and the deep wind driving him
farther and farther were like desire.
And if his enemies crouched in the moonlight,
he did not notice them,
nor did he notice the owl staring into his limbs,
nor feel the moth pressing against his ribs
as if he were the only light.
And he did not hear the cry that would always be with him,
that rose from his throat like a name
beginning to shape the sound of its being.
He wanted to learn the lessons of dark,
and he wanted the sheets of morning to take him in.
He wanted both, and woke
unable to say the one thing he would try to remember.

3

It was early.
She stood over him, offering him coffee.
She asked him what he was trying to say.
There was no way to tell her what he had not said.
His voice would fail to convey what it was,
and his silence would fail to suggest its absence.

He remembered the driving wind
and the way he waved into the dark
and how the distance kept welcoming him.
He wished she had not asked.
He imagined that he had wakened in the wrong house,
that he would leave, that he would go back.
And he drifted off to sleep.
If he had gone before, he did not know it now.
The clouds moving slowly over the lake,
the failed brilliance of daylight,
seemed too much a part of the present.
He went from field to field,
each one blank with possibility,
each one darkening with disappointment.
As he went he felt the acuteness of his passion.
He walked because he had to,
and when he looked up, the sky was empty
and the world seemed cleared of meaning.
Once again, he tried to say something,
but he awoke.

4

She stood over him.
She said she had watched him,
that he had been trying to say something.
He had nothing to say.
He lay on the couch with his eyes open.
Sometimes he did not know if he slept
or just thought about sleep. He knew
that he would lie down and the journey would begin.
If it was another life, it was not the one which lasted.
He would have to come back

and recapture what he had left.
He would offer himself as hostage
and the life he woke into would take him.
How long would it last?
When he closed his eyes, the clouds had gone,
the sun had turned everything white.
Even if he became less than he was and the terrain
became harsher, even if no trace remained
of his having been, he would keep going.
He felt he had given up the visible world,
that the sun had turned everything white to prepare his way.
He walked in the harsh light,
and when he stopped he discovered
he was standing beside someone who wore clothes like his
and whose face was like his own and who asked,
Where am I? Where am I going?
He tried to answer but the cloud of his voice would say nothing.
He wanted to know who the man was.
He tried to think of his name, but again he woke.

5

She watched him open his eyes
and asked him what he had said about a name.
He tried to remember where he was going.
Was he looking for someone?
The light came in the windows,
erasing the furniture, turning
the room white. He saw nothing.
And he remembered how she would dress and undress
and how he would wait in bed, watching her.
All night he would feel her beside him,
her breathing moved through his dreams

and shook him like nothing else.
He had traveled a great distance since then
and did not know where he was going.
She told him the coffee was getting cold.
He closed his eyes.
The journey was not what he wanted.
Each day was too long, and not long enough
to endure himself in. And there was nothing ahead.
The stranger had gone and there was
no lake or fields or woods.
The sun's brightness fell and he continued,
his ignorance shining, his failure
finding him out and leading him on.
Survival was motion and he could not stop.

6

She sat in a chair across the room, staring at him.
It was not a bad life, he thought
as he sipped the cold coffee
and she moved into a closer chair.
Still, he could not speak.
She would leave the room and change
into a cooler dress, a warmer dress.
She might even take a trip.
She leaned over him. She said she'd been watching him,
was there something he wanted to tell her?
He knew she would meet somebody.
He knew she would leave him.
He tried to tell her to stay but it was no use.
His mouth was dry and the sun was white
and he could not take another step.
He tried to call, but could not remember the name.

He stood in the absence of what he had known
and waited, and when he woke
the room was empty. The light had turned
and the chair she had sat in was covered with dust.
He had been gone a long time
and now the journey was over.
Without her he would not be able to sleep,
and there was no more to say,
and even if there were, he would not say it.

THE UNTELLING

He leaned forward over the paper
and for a long time saw nothing.
Then, slowly, the lake opened
like a white eye
and he was a child
playing with his cousins,
and there was a lawn
and a row of trees
that went to the water.
It was a warm afternoon in August
and there was a party
about to begin.
He leaned forward over the paper
and he wrote:

I waited with my cousins across the lake,
watching the grown-ups walking on the far side
along the bank shaded by elms. It was hot.
The sky was clear. My cousins and I stood
for hours among the heavy branches, watching
our parents, and it seemed as if nothing would enter
their lives to make them change, not even the man
running over the lawn, waving a sheet
of paper and shouting. They moved beyond the claims
of weather, beyond whatever news there was,
and did not see the dark begin to deepen
in the trees and bushes, and rise in the folds
of their own dresses and in the stiff white
of their own shirts. Waves of laughter carried
over the water where we, the children, were watching.

It was a scene that was not ours. We were
too far away, and soon we would leave.

He leaned back.
How could he know
the scene was not his?
The summer was with him,
the voices had returned and he saw the faces.
The day had started before the party;
it had rained in the morning
and suddenly cleared in time.
The hems of the dresses were wet.
The men's shoes glistened.
There was a cloud shaped like a hand
which kept lowering.
There was no way to know
why there were times that afternoon
the lawn seemed empty, or why even then
the voices of the grown-ups lingered there.
He took what he had written
and put it aside.
He sat down and began again:

We all went down to the lake, over the lawn,
walking, not saying a word. All the way
from the house, along the shade cast by the elms.
And the sun bore down, lifting the dampness, allowing
the lake to shine like a clear plate surrounded
by mist. We sat and stared at the water and then
lay down on the grass and slept. The air turned colder.
The wind shook the trees. We lay so long we imagined
a hand brushing the fallen leaves from our faces.

But it was not autumn, and some of us, the youngest,
got up and went to the other side of the lake
and stared at the men and women asleep; the men
in stiff white shirts, the women in pale dresses.
We watched all afternoon. And a man ran down
from the house, shouting, waving a sheet of paper.
And the sleepers rose as if nothing had happened,
as if the night had not begun to move
into the trees. We heard their laughter, then
their sighs. They lay back down, and the dark came over
the lawn and covered them. As far as we know
they are still there, their arms crossed over their chests,
their stiff clothing creased. We have never been back.

He looked at what he had written.
How far had he come?
And why had it grown dark just then?
And wasn't he alone when he watched the others
lie down on the lawn?
He stared out the window,
hoping the people at the lake,
the lake itself, would fade.
He wanted to move beyond his past.
He thought of the man
running over the lawn who seemed familiar.
He looked at what he had written
and wondered how he had crossed the lake,
and if his cousins went with him.
Had someone called?
Had someone waved goodbye?
What he had written told him nothing.
He put it away and began again:

I waited under the trees in front of the house,
thinking of nothing, watching the sunlight wash
over the roof. I heard nothing, felt
nothing, even when she appeared in a long
yellow dress, pointed white shoes, her hair
drawn back in a tight bun; even when
she took my hand and led me along the row
of tall trees toward the lake where the rest had gathered,
the men in their starched shirts, the women in
their summer dresses, the children watching the water.
Even then, my life seemed far away
as though it were waiting for me to discover it.
She held my hand and led me toward the water.
The hem of her dress was wet. She said nothing
when she left me with my cousins and joined
the others who stood together. I knew by the way
they talked that something would happen, that some of us,
the youngest, would go away that afternoon
and never find the way back. As I walked through the woods
to the other side of the lake, their voices faded
in the breaking of leaves and branches underfoot.
Though I walked away, I had no sense of going.
I sat and watched the scene across the lake,
I watched and did nothing. Small waves of laughter
carried over the water and then died down.
I was not moved. Even when the man
ran across the lawn, shouting, I did nothing.
It seemed as if the wind drew the dark
from the trees onto the grass. The adults stood
together. They would never leave that shore.
I watched the one in the yellow dress whose name
I had begun to forget and who waited with

the others and who stared at where I was
but could not see me. Already the full moon
had risen and dropped its white ashes on the lake.
And the woman and the others slowly began
to take off their clothes, and the mild rushes of wind
rinsed their skin, their pale bodies shone
briefly among the shadows until they lay
on the damp grass. And the children had all gone.
And that was all. And even then I felt
nothing. I knew that I would never see
the woman in the yellow dress again,
and that the scene by the lake would not be repeated,
and that that summer would be a place too distant
for me ever to find myself in again.
Although I have tried to return, I have always
ended here, where I am now. The lake
still exists, and so does the lawn, though the people
who slept there that afternoon have not been seen since.

It bothered him,
as if too much had been said.
He would have preferred
the lake without a story,
or no story and no lake.
His pursuit was a form of evasion:
the more he tried to uncover
the more there was to conceal
the less he understood.
If he kept it up,
he would lose everything.
He knew this
and remembered what he could—
always at a distance,

on the other side of the lake,
or across the lawn,
always vanishing, always there.
And the woman and the others would save him
and he would save them.
He put his hand on the paper.
He would write a letter for the man
running across the lawn.
He would say what he knew.
He rested his head in his arms and tried to sleep.
He knew that night had once come,
that something had once happened.
He wanted to know but not to know.
Maybe something had happened
one afternoon in August.
Maybe he was there or waiting to be there,
waiting to come running across a lawn
to a lake where people were staring
across the water.
He would come running
and be too late.
The people there would be asleep.
Their children would be watching them.
He would bring what he had written
and then would lie down with the others.
He would be the man
he had become, the man
who would run across the lawn.
He began again:

I sat in the house that looked down on the lake,
the lawn, the woods beside the lawn. I heard
the children near the shore, their voices lifted

where no memory of the place would reach.
I watched the women, the men in white, strolling
in the August heat. I shut the window
and saw them in the quiet glass, passing
each time farther away. The trees began
to darken and the children left. I saw
the distant water fade in the gray shade
of grass and underbrush across the lake.
I thought I saw the children sitting, watching
their parents in a slow parade along
the shore. The shapes among the trees kept changing.
It may have been one child I saw, its face.
It may have been my own face looking back.
I felt myself descend into the future.
I saw beyond the lawn, beyond the lake,
beyond the waiting dark, the end of summer,
the end of autumn, the icy air, the silence,
and then, again, the windowpane. I was
where I was, where I would be, and where I am.
I watched the men and women as the white
eye of the lake began to close and deepen
into blue, then into black. It was too late
for them to call the children. They lay on the grass
and the wind blew and shook the first leaves loose.
I wanted to tell them something. I saw myself
running, waving a sheet of paper, shouting,
telling them all that I had something to give them,
but when I got there, they were gone.

He looked up from the paper
and saw himself in the window.
It was an August night
and he was tired,

and the trees swayed
and the wind shook the window.
It was late.
It did not matter.
He would never catch up
with his past. His life
was slowing down.
It was going.
He could feel it,
could hear it in his speech.
It sounded like nothing,
yet he would pass it on.
And his children would live in it
and they would pass it on,
and it would always sound
like hope dying, like space opening,
like a lawn, or a lake,
or an afternoon.
And pain could not give it
the meaning it lacked;
there was no pain,
only disappearance.
Why had he begun in the first place?
He was tired,
and gave himself up to sleep,
and slept where he was,
and slept without dreaming,
so that when he woke
it seemed as if nothing had happened.
The lake opened like a white eye,
the elms rose over the lawn,
the sun over the elms.
It was as he remembered it—

the mist, the dark, the heat,
the woods on the other side.
He sat for a long time
and saw that they had come
and were on the lawn.
They were waiting for him,
staring up at the window.
The wind blew their hair
and they made no motion.
He was afraid to follow them.
He knew what would happen.
He knew the children would wander off,
that he would lie down with their parents.
And he was afraid.
When they turned
and walked down to the lake
into the shade cast by the elms
the children did wander off.
He saw them in the distance,
across the lake, and wondered if one
would come back someday
and be where he was now.
He saw the adults on the lawn,
beginning to lie down.
And he wanted to warn them,
to tell them what he knew.
He ran from the house down to the lake,
knowing that he would be late,
that he would be left
to continue.
When he got there,
they were gone,
and he was alone in the dark,

unable to speak.
He stood still.
He felt the world recede
into the clouds,
into the shelves of air.
He closed his eyes.
He thought of the lake,
the closets of weeds.
He thought of the moth asleep
in the dust of its wings,
of the bat hanging in the caves of trees.
He felt himself at that moment to be
more than his need to survive,
more than his losses,
because he was less than anything.
He swayed back and forth.
The silence was in him
and it rose like joy,
like the beginning.
When he opened his eyes,
the silence had spread, the sheets
of darkness seemed endless,
the sheets he held in his hand.
He turned and walked to the house.
He went to the room
that looked out on the lawn.
He sat and began to write:

THE UNTELLING

To the Woman in the Yellow Dress

THE LATE HOUR

I   *Another Place*

THE COMING OF LIGHT

Even this late it happens:
the coming of love, the coming of light.
You wake and the candles are lit as if by themselves,
stars gather, dreams pour into your pillows,
sending up warm bouquets of air.
Even this late the bones of the body shine
and tomorrow's dust flares into breath.

ANOTHER PLACE

I walk
into what light
there is

not enough for blindness
or clear sight
of what is to come

yet I see
the water
the single boat
the man standing

he is not someone I know

this is another place
what light there is
spreads like a net
over nothing

what is to come
has come to this
before

this is the mirror
in which pain is asleep
this is the country
nobody visits

LINES FOR WINTER

for Ros Krauss

Tell yourself
as it gets cold and gray falls from the air
that you will go on
walking, hearing
the same tune no matter where
you find yourself—
inside the dome of dark
or under the cracking white
of the moon's gaze in a valley of snow.
Tonight as it gets cold
tell yourself
what you know which is nothing
but the tune your bones play
as you keep going. And you will be able
for once to lie down under the small fire
of winter stars.
And if it happens that you cannot
go on or turn back
and you find yourself
where you will be at the end,
tell yourself
in that final flowing of cold through your limbs
that you love what you are.

MY SON

My son,
my only son,
the one I never had,
would be a man today.

He moves
in the wind,
fleshless, nameless.
Sometimes

he comes
and leans his head,
lighter than air
against my shoulder

and I ask him,
Son,
where do you stay,
where do you hide?

And he answers me
with a cold breath,
You never noticed
though I called

and called
and keep on calling
from a place
beyond,

beyond love,
where nothing,
everything,
wants to be born.

(AFTER CARLOS DRUMMOND DE ANDRADE)

WHITE

for Harold Bloom

Now in the middle of my life
all things are white.
I walk under the trees,
the frayed leaves,
the wide net of noon,
and the day is white.
And my breath is white,
drifting over the patches
of grass and fields of ice
into the high circles of light.
As I walk, the darkness of
my steps is also white,
and my shadow blazes
under me. In all seasons
the silence where I find myself
and what I make of nothing are white,
the white of sorrow,
the white of death.
Even the night that calls
like a dark wish is white;
and in my sleep as I turn
in the weather of dreams
it is the white of my sheets
and white shades of the moon
drawn over my floor
that save me for morning.
And out of my waking
the circle of light widens,
it fills with trees, houses,
stretches of ice.

It reaches out. It rings
the eye with white.
All things are one.
All things are joined
even beyond the edge of sight.

FOR JESSICA, MY DAUGHTER

Tonight I walked,
lost in my own meditation,
and was afraid,
not of the labyrinth
that I have made of love and self
but of the dark and faraway.
I walked, hearing the wind in the trees,
feeling the cold against my skin,
but what I dwelled on
were the stars blazing
in the immense arc of sky.

Jessica, it is so much easier
to think of our lives,
as we move under the brief luster of leaves,
loving what we have,
than to think of how it is
such small beings as we
travel in the dark
with no visible way
or end in sight.

Yet there were times I remember
under the same sky
when the body's bones became light
and the wound of the skull
opened to receive
the cold rays of the cosmos,
and were, for an instant,
themselves the cosmos,

there were times when I could believe
we were the children of stars
and our words were made of the same
dust that flames in space,
times when I could feel in the lightness of breath
the weight of a whole day
come to rest.

But tonight
it is different.
Afraid of the dark
in which we drift or vanish altogether,
I imagine a light
that would not let us stray too far apart,
a secret moon or mirror,
a sheet of paper,
something you could carry
in the dark
when I am away.

II   *From the Long Sad Party*

FROM THE LONG SAD PARTY

Someone was saying
something about shadows covering the field, about
how things pass, how one sleeps toward morning
and the morning goes.

Someone was saying
how the wind dies down but comes back,
how shells are the coffins of wind
but the weather continues.

It was a long night
and someone said something about the moon shedding its white
on the cold field, that there was nothing ahead
but more of the same.

Someone mentioned
a city she had been in before the war, a room with two candles
against a wall, someone dancing, someone watching.
We began to believe

the night would not end.
Someone was saying the music was over and no one had noticed.
Then someone said something about the planets, about the stars,
how small they were, how far away.

THE LATE HOUR

A man walks toward town,
a slack breeze smelling of earth
and the raw green of trees blows at his back.

He drags the weight of his passion as if nothing were over,
as if the woman, now curled in bed beside her lover,
still cared for him.

She is awake and stares at scars of light
trapped in the panes of glass.
He stands under her window, calling her name;

he calls all night and it makes no difference.
It will happen again, he will come back wherever she is.
Again he will stand outside and imagine

her eyes opening in the dark
and see her rise to the window and peer down.
Again she will lie awake beside her lover

and hear the voice from somewhere in the dark.
Again the late hour, the moon and stars,
the wounds of night that heal without sound,

again the luminous wind of morning that comes before the sun.
And, finally, without warning or desire,
the lonely and the feckless end.

SEVEN DAYS

FIRST DAY

I sat in a room that was almost dark,
looking out to sea. There was a light on the water
that released a rainbow which landed near the stairs.
I was surprised to discover you at the end of it.

SECOND DAY

I sat in a beach chair surrounded by tall grass
so that only the top of my hat showed.
The sky kept shifting but the sunlight stayed.
It was a glass pillar filled with bright dust, and you were inside.

THIRD DAY

A comet with two tails appeared. You were between them
with your arms outspread as if you were keeping the tails apart.
I wished you would speak but you didn't. I knew then
that you might remain silent forever.

FOURTH DAY

This evening in my room there was a pool of pink light
that floated on the wooden floor and I thought of the night
you sailed away. I closed my eyes and tried to think
of ways we might be reconciled; I could not think of one.

FIFTH DAY

A light appeared and I thought the dawn had come.
But the light was in the mirror and became brighter
the closer I moved. You were staring at me.
I watched you until morning but you never spoke.

SIXTH DAY

It was in the afternoon but I was sure
there was moonlight trapped under the plates.
You were standing outside the window, saying, "Lift them up."
When I lifted them up the sea was dark,
the wind was from the west, and you were gone.

SEVENTH DAY

I went for a walk late at night wondering whether
you would come back. The air was warm and the odor of roses
made me think of the day you appeared in my room,
in a pool of light. Soon the moon would rise
and I hoped you would come. In the meantime I thought
of the old stars falling and the ashes of one thing and another.
I knew that I would be scattered among them,
that the dream of light would continue without me,
for it was never my dream, it was yours. And it was clear
in the dark of the seventh night that my time would come soon.
I looked at the hill, I looked out over the calm water.
Already the moon was rising and you were here.

ABOUT A MAN

Would get up at night,
go to the mirror and ask:
Who's here?

Would turn, sink to his knees
and stare at snow falling blameless
in the night air.

Would cry:
Heaven, look down!
See? No one is here.

Would take off his clothes and say:
My flesh is a grave with nothing inside.

Would lean to the mirror:
You there, you, wake me,
tell me none of what I've said is true.

THE STORY

It is the old story: complaints about the moon
sinking into the sea, about stars in the first light fading,
about the lawn wet with dew, the lawn silver, the lawn cold.

It goes on and on: a man stares at his shadow
and says it's the ash of himself falling away, says his days
are the real black holes in space. But none of it's true.

You know the one I mean: it's the one about the minutes dying,
and the hours, and the years; it's the story I tell
about myself, about you, about everyone.

FOR HER

Let it be anywhere
on any night you wish,
in your room that is empty and dark

or down the street
or at those dim frontiers
you barely see, barely dream of.

You will not feel desire,
nothing will warn you,
no sudden wind, no stillness of air.

She will appear,
looking like someone you knew:
the friend who wasted her life,

the girl who sat under the palm tree.
Her bracelets will glitter,
becoming the lights

of a village you turned from years ago.

SO YOU SAY

It is all in the mind, you say, and has
nothing to do with happiness. The coming of cold,
the coming of heat, the mind has all the time in the world.
I wish the bottom of things were not so far away.

You take my arm and say something will happen,
something unusual for which we were always prepared,
like the sun arriving after a day in Asia,
like the moon departing after a night with us.

POEMS OF AIR

The poems of air are slowly dying;
too light for the page, too faint, too far away,
the ones we've called The Moon, The Stars, The Sun,
sink into the sea or slide behind the cooling trees
at the field's edge. The grave of light is everywhere.

Some summer day or winter night the poems will cease.
No one will weep, no one will look at the sky.
A heavy mist will fill the valleys,
an indelible dark will rain on the hills,
and nothing, not a single bird, will sing.

AN OLD MAN AWAKE IN HIS OWN DEATH

This is the place that was promised
when I went to sleep,
taken from me when I woke.

This is the place unknown to anyone,
where names of ships and stars
drift out of reach.

The mountains are not mountains anymore;
the sun is not the sun.
One tends to forget how it was;

I see myself, I see
the shine of darkness on my brow.
Once I was whole, once I was young . . .

As if it mattered now
and you could hear me
and the weather of this place would ever cease.

NO PARTICULAR DAY

Items of no
particular day
swarm down—

moves of the mind
that never quite
make it as poems:

like the way
you take me aside
and leave me

by the water
with its waves
knitted

like your sweater
like your brow;
moves of the mind

that take us
somewhere near
and leave us

combing the air
for signs
of change,

signs the sky
will break
and shower down

upon us
particular
ideas of light.

EXILES

Only they had escaped
to tell us how
the house had gone
and things had vanished,
how they lay in their beds
and were wakened by the wind
and saw the roof gone
and thought they were dreaming.
But the starry night
and the chill they felt were real.
And they looked around
and saw trees instead of walls.
When the sun rose
they saw nothing of their own.
Other houses were collapsing.
Other trees were falling.
They ran for the train
but the train had gone.
They ran to the river
but there were no boats.
They thought about us.
They would come here.
So they got to their feet
and started to run.
There were no birds.
The wind had died.
Their clothes were tattered

and fell to the ground.
So they ran
and covered themselves
with their hands
and shut their eyes
and imagined us
taking them in.
They could not hear
the sound of their footsteps.
They felt they were drifting.
All day they had run
and now could see nothing,
not even their hands.
Everything faded
around their voices
until only their voices were left,
telling the story.
And after the story,
their voices were gone.

2

They were not gone
and the story they told
was barely begun,
for when the air was silent
and everything faded
it meant only that these
exiles came
into a country
not their own,
into a radiance
without hope.

Having come too far,
they were frightened back
into the night of their origin.
And on their way back
they heard the footsteps
and felt the warmth
of the clothes they thought
had been lifted from them.
They ran by the boats at anchor,
hulking in the bay,
by the train waiting
under the melting frost of stars.
Their sighs were mixed
with the sighs of the wind.
And when the moon rose,
they were still going back.
And when the trees
and houses reappeared,
they saw what they wanted:
the return of their story
to where it began.
They saw it in the cold
room under the roof
chilled by moonlight.
They lay in their beds
and the shadows of the giant trees
brushed darkly against the walls.

III   *Poor North*

POOR NORTH

It is cold, the snow is deep,
the wind beats around in its cage of trees,
clouds have the look of rags torn and soiled with use,
and starlings peck at the ice.
It is north, poor north. Nothing goes right.

The man of the house has gone to work,
selling chairs and sofas in a failing store.
His wife stays home and stares from the window into the trees,
trying to recall the life she lost, though it wasn't much.
White flowers of frost build up on the glass.

It is late in the day. Brants and Canada geese are asleep
on the waters of St. Margaret's Bay.
The man and his wife are out for a walk; see how they lean
into the wind; they turn up their collars
and the small puffs of their breath are carried away.

WHERE ARE THE WATERS OF CHILDHOOD?

See where the windows are boarded up,
where the gray siding shines in the sun and salt air
and the asphalt shingles on the roof have peeled or fallen off,
where tiers of oxeye daisies float on a sea of grass?
That's the place to begin.

Enter the kingdom of rot,
smell the damp plaster, step over the shattered glass,
the pockets of dust, the rags, the soiled remains of a mattress,
look at the rusted stove and sink, at the rectangular stain
on the wall where Winslow Homer's *Gulf Stream* hung.

Go to the room where your father and mother
would let themselves go in the drift and pitch of love,
and hear, if you can, the creak of their bed,
then go to the place where you hid.

Go to your room, to all the rooms whose cold, damp air you breathed,
to all the unwanted places where summer, fall, winter, spring,
seem the same unwanted season, where the trees you knew have died
and other trees have risen. Visit that other place
you barely recall, that other house half hidden.

See the two dogs burst into sight. When you leave,
they will cease, snuffed out in the glare of an earlier light.
Visit the neighbors down the block; he waters his lawn,
she sits on her porch, but not for long.
When you look again they are gone.

Keep going back, back to the field, flat and sealed in mist,
green the color of light sinking in ice. On the other side,
a man and a woman are waiting; they have come back,
your mother before she was gray, your father before he was white.

Now look at the North West Arm, how it glows a deep cerulean blue.
See the light on the grass, the one leaf burning, the cloud
that flares. You're almost there, in a moment your parents
will disappear, leaving you under the light of a vanished star,
under the dark of a star newly born. Now is the time.

Now you invent the boat of your flesh and set it upon the waters
and drift in the gradual swell, in the laboring salt.
Now you look down. The waters of childhood are there.

POT ROAST

I gaze upon the roast,
that is sliced and laid out
on my plate
and over it
I spoon the juices
of carrot and onion.
And for once I do not regret
the passage of time.

I sit by a window
that looks
on the soot-stained brick of buildings
and do not care that I see
no living thing—not a bird,
not a branch in bloom,
not a soul moving
in the rooms
behind the dark panes.
These days when there is little
to love or to praise
one could do worse
than yield
to the power of food.
So I bend

to inhale
the steam that rises
from my plate, and I think
of the first time
I tasted a roast

like this.
It was years ago
in Seabright,
Nova Scotia;
my mother leaned
over my dish and filled it
and when I finished
filled it again.
I remember the gravy,
its odor of garlic and celery,
and sopping it up
with pieces of bread.

And now
I taste it again.
The meat of memory.
The meat of no change.
I raise my fork in praise,
and I eat.

THE HOUSE IN FRENCH VILLAGE

for Elizabeth Bishop

It stood by itself
in a sloping field,
it was white
with green
shutters and trim,

and its gambrel roof
gave it the look
of a small
prim barn.
From the porch

when the weather was clear,
I could see Fox Point,
across the bay
where the fishermen,
I was told,

laid out
their catch of tuna
on the pier
and hacked away with axes
at the bellies

of the giant fish.
I would stare
at Wedge Island
where gulls wheeled
in loud broken rings

above their young;
at Albert Hubley's shack
built over water, and sagging;
at Boutelier's wharf
loaded down

with barrels of brine
and nets to be mended.
I would sit
with my grandmother,
my aunt, and my mother,

the four of us rocking
in chairs, watching
the narrow dirt road
for a sign
of the black

baby Austin
my father would drive
to town and back.
But the weather
was not often clear

and all we could see
were sheets of cold rain
sweeping this way and that,
riffling the sea's coat
of deep green,

and the wind
beating the field flat,
sending up to the porch
gusts of salt spray
that carried

the odor of fish
and the rot,
so it seemed,
of the whole bay,
while we kept watch.

THE GARDEN

for Robert Penn Warren

It shines in the garden,
in the white foliage of the chestnut tree,
in the brim of my father's hat
as he walks on the gravel.

In the garden suspended in time
my mother sits in a redwood chair;
light fills the sky,
the folds of her dress,
the roses tangled beside her.

And when my father bends
to whisper in her ear,
when they rise to leave
and the swallows dip and dart
and the moon and stars
have drifted off together, it shines.

Even as you lean over this page,
late and alone, it shines; even now
in the moment before it disappears.

SNOWFALL

Watching snow cover the ground, cover itself,
cover everything that is not you, you see
it is the downward drift of light
upon the sound of air sweeping away the air,
it is the fall of moments into moments, the burial
of sleep, the down of winter, the negative of night.

IV   *Night Pieces*

NIGHT PIECES

for Bill and Sandy Bailey

I

A fine bright moon and thousands of stars!
It is a still night, a very still night
and the stillness is everywhere.

Not only is it a still night
on deserted roads and hilltops
where the dim, quilted countryside seems to doze
as it fans out into clumps of trees dark and unbending
against the sky, with the gray dust of moonlight upon them,

not only is it a still night
in backyards overgrown with weeds, and in woods,
and by tracks where the rat sleeps under the garnet-crusted rock,
and in the abandoned station that reeks of mildew and urine,
and on the river where the oil slick rides the current
sparkling among islands and scattered weirs,

not only is it a still night
where the river winds through marshes and mudflats fouled
by bottles, tires and rusty cans, and where it narrows
through the sloping acres of higher ground covered with plots
cleared and graded for building,

not only is it a still night
wherever the river flows, where houses cluster in small towns,
but farther down where more and more bridges are reflected in it,
where wharves, cranes, warehouses, make it black and awful,
where it turns from those creaking shapes and mingles with the sea,

and not only is it a still night
at sea and on the pale glass of the beach
where the watcher stands upright in the mystery and motion of his life
and sees the silent ships move in from nowhere he has ever been,
crossing the path of light that he believes runs only to him,

but even in this stranger's wilderness of a city
it is a still night. Steeples and skyscrapers grow
more ethereal, rooftops crowded with towers and ducts
lose their ugliness under the shining of the urban moon;
street noises are fewer and are softened, and footsteps
on the sidewalks pass more quietly away.

In this place where the sound of sirens never ceases
and people move like a ghostly traffic from home to work and home,
and the poor in their tenements speak to their gods
and the rich do not hear them, every sound is merged,
this moonlit night, into a distant humming, as if
the city, finally, were singing itself to sleep.

(AFTER DICKENS)

II

It is night. I feel it is night
not because darkness has fallen
(what do I care about darkness falling)
but because down in myself the shouting
has stopped, has given up.
I feel we are night,
that we sink into dark
and dissolve into night.
I feel it is night in the wind,
night in the sea, in the stone,
in the harp of the angel who sings to me.
And turning on lights wouldn't help,
and taking my hand wouldn't help. Not now.
It is night where Jess lies down,
where Phil and Fran are asleep,
night for the Simics, night for the Baileys,
night for Dan, for Richard, for Sandy.
For all my friends it is night,
and in all my friends it is night.
It is night, not death, it is night
filling up sleep without dreams,
without stars. It is night,
not pain or rest, it is night,
the perfection of night.
It is night that changes

now in the first glimpse of day,
in the ribbons of rising light,
and the world assembles itself once more.
In the park someone is running,
someone is walking his dog.
For whatever reason, people are waking.
Someone is cooking, someone
is bringing *The Times* to the door.
Streets are filling with light.
My friends are rubbing the sleep from their eyes.
Jules is rubbing the sleep from her eyes,
and I sit at the table
drinking my morning coffee.
All that we lost at night is back.

Thank you, faithful things!
Thank you, world!
To know that the city is still there,
that the woods are still there,
and the houses, and the humming of traffic
and the slow cows grazing in the field;
that the earth continues to turn
and time hasn't stopped,
that we come back whole
to suck the sweet marrow of day,
thank you, bright morning,
thank you, thank you!

(AFTER CARLOS DRUMMOND DE ANDRADE)

THE MONUMENT

To the translator of
The Monument
in the future:
"Siste Viator"

1

Let me introduce myself. I am . . . and so on and so forth. Now you know more about me than I know about you.

2

I am setting out from the meeting with what I am, with what I now begin to be, my descendant and my ancestor, my father and my son, my unlike likeness.

Though I am reaching over hundreds of years as if they did not exist, imagining you at this moment trying to imagine me, and proving finally that imagination accomplishes more than history, you know me better than I know you. Maybe my voice is dim as it reaches over so many years, so many that they seem one long blur erased and joined by events and lives that become one event, one life; even so, my voice is sufficient to make The Monument out of this moment.

3

And just as there are areas of our soul which flower and give fruit only beneath the gaze of some spirit come from the eternal region to which they belong in time, just so, when that gaze is hidden from us by absence, these areas long for that magical gaze like the earth longing for the sun so that it may give out flowering plants and fruit.

> *Shine alone, shine nakedly, shine like bronze,*
> *that reflects neither my face nor any inner part*
> *of my being, shine like fire, that mirrors nothing.*

Why have I chosen this way to continue myself under your continuing gaze? I might have had my likeness carved in stone, but it is not my image that I want you to have, nor my life, nor the life around me, only this document. What I include of myself is unreal and distracting. Only this luminous moment has life, this instant in which we both write, this flash of voice.

4

Look in thy glass, and tell the face thou viewest
Now is the time that face should form another . . .

Many would have thought it an Happiness to have had their lot of Life in some notable Conjunctures of Ages past; but the uncertainty of future Times hath tempted few to make a part in Ages to come.

And the secret of human life, the universal secret, the root secret from which all other secrets spring, is the longing for more life, the furious and insatiable desire to be everything else without ever ceasing to be ourselves, to take possession of the entire universe without letting the universe take possession of us and absorb us; it is the desire to be someone else without ceasing to be myself, and continue being myself at the same time I am someone else. . . .

It is a struggle to believe I am writing to someone else, to you, when I imagine the spectral conditions of your existence. This work has allowed you to exist, yet this work exists because you are translating it. Am I wrong? It must be early morning as you write. You sit in a large, barely furnished room with one window from which you can see a gray body of water on which several black ducks are asleep. How still the world is so many years from now. How few people there are. They never leave town, never visit the ruins of the great city.

5

Or let me put it this way. You must imagine that you are the author of this work, that the wind is blowing from the northeast, bringing rain that slaps and spatters against your windows. You must imagine the ocean's swash and backwash sounding hushed and muffled. Imagine a long room with a light at one end, illuminating a desk, a chair, papers. Imagine someone is in the chair. Imagine he is you; it is long ago and you are dressed in the absurd clothes of the time. You must imagine yourself asking the question: which of us has sought the other?

6

I have no rest from myself. I feel as though I am devouring my whole life. . . .

O my soul, I gave you all, and I have emptied all my hands to you; and now—now you say to me, smiling and full of melancholy, "Which of us has to be thankful? Should not the giver be thankful that the receiver received? Is not giving a need? Is not receiving a mercy?"

All voice is but echo caught from a soundless voice.

In what language do I live? I live in none. I live in you. It is your voice that I begin to hear and it has no language. I hear the motions of a spirit, and the sound of what is secret becomes, for me, a voice that is your voice speaking in my ear. It is a misery unheard of to know the secret has no name, no language I can learn.

7

O if you knew! If you knew! How it has been. How the ladies of the house would talk softly in the moonlight under the orange trees of the courtyard, impressing upon me the sweetness of their voices and something mysterious in the quietude of their lives. O the heaviness of that air, the perfume of jasmine, pale lights against the stones of the courtyard walls. Monument! Monument! How will you ever know!

8

Then do thy office, Muse; I teach thee how
To make him seem, long hence, as he shows now.

Through you I shall be born again; myself again and again; myself without others; myself with a tomb; myself beyond death. I imagine you taking my name; I imagine you saying "myself myself" again and again. And suddenly there will be no blue sky or sun or shape of anything without that simple utterance.

9

. . . Nothing must stand

Between you and the shapes you take
When the crust of shape has been destroyed.

You as you are? You are yourself.

It has been necessary to submit to vacancy in order to begin again, to clear ground, to make space. I can allow nothing to be received. Therein lies my triumph *and* my mediocrity. Nothing is the destiny of everyone, it is our commonness made dumb. I am passing it on. The Monument is a void, artless and everlasting. What I was I am no longer. I speak for nothing, the nothing that I am, the nothing that is this work. And you shall perpetuate me not in the name of what I was, but in the name of what I am.

10

Perhaps there is no monument and this is invisible writing that has appeared in fate's corridor; you are no mere translator but an interpreter-angel.

11

I begin to sense your impatience. It is hard for you to believe that I am what you were. It is a barren past that I represent—one that would have you be its sole guardian. But consider how often we are given to invent ourselves; maybe once, but even so we say we are another, another entirely similar.

12

Stories are told of people who die and after a moment come back to life, telling of a radiance and deep calm they experienced. I too died once but said nothing until this moment, not wishing to upset my friends or to allow my enemies jokes about whether I was really alive to begin with. It happened a couple of years ago in March or April. I was having coffee. I know I was dead just a few minutes because the coffee was still warm when I came back. I saw no light, felt no radiance. I saw my life flash before me as a succession of meals and I felt full. This feeling was to give way to an image of waste. How much would be lost! A box placed underground with me inside would never be right. And then I thought of The Monument. It was this promise of adequate memorial that brought me back to life, to my room and my coffee.

13

Stars denote places where The Monument has been reported.

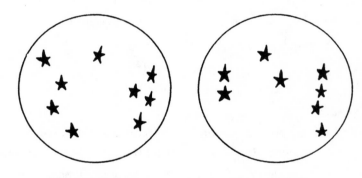

Eastern Hemisphere   Western Hemisphere

14

It may be wise at this time to get down to practical matters, to make suggestions that will ease your task. There are words that I use, words used often in the poetry of my day, which should not constrain you. It is possible that they will not exist in your time or in your language. In either case, find words for which you yourself have a fondness. If this is difficult, then I suggest you use one word to cover the many. The objects you see from where you sit may be "anything." "Anything" may be "nothing," depending on what your feeling is. If "nothing" conveys the wrong idea, use "something." By all means, use "something" if you agree with the poet who shrieks, "There is not nothing, no, no, never nothing."

15

The certainty of death is attended by uncertainties, in time, manner, places. The variety of Monuments hath often obscured true graves: and Cenotaphs confounded Sepulchres.

The true Monument must survive, must stand by itself despite the possible survival of false monuments. Do not be taken in by structures that call themselves The Monument and look like this:

THE MONUMENT

During the night
a storm broke,
striking the monument,
sending it down,
stone and green
pieces of bronze,
onto the lawn.
Now it lies
among shrubs
and torn limbs
of trees. You scrape
the pieces clean,
cracks and channels
made by rain, you scrub
away the scars, stains,
names painted

on the pedestal.
When you are done,
nothing about
the monument
will look the same.
The cape will gleam,
curls of hair
will seem to swirl
in the moonlight
or spill
in the bright sun.
No wind will scream
under the arms or chin;
all signs and syllables
of pain will be
rephrased, and when
you leave the monument's
hard gaze, the cold
violet of its shade,
you will not think
of turning back.
Not even fears
of slow decay,
of fires blazing
at its base
will keep you there.
Before you walk away,
you will drop a list
inside its throat
of what to do in case
it falls again.
Your final say

buried in the monument's
cold shape . . .

16

Or look like this:

THE MONUMENT

You will see it
in the shade or covered
with a shawl
of sunlight or sheen
of wet gray;
or later, barely
visible while
the night passes
with its silent cargo
of moons and stars.
You will see sleeping
figures at its feet;
you will see
in its bleached eyes
baked by sun,
strafed by rain,
the meanness of
the sky; and in
its barely open mouth
perpetual twilight.
You will see it
when you come
and when you leave,

you will see it
when you do not wish to
and you will never know
whose monument it is
or why it came to you . . .

17

How sad it is to come back to one's work, so much less than the world it masks or echoes or reminds one of. Such dreariness to return to one's singleness, one's simple reductions. Poems have come to seem so little. Even The Monument is little. How it wishes it were something it cannot be—its own perpetual birth instead of its death again and again, each sentence a memorial.

18

If you want me again look for me under your bootsoles.

> *Who walks where I am not,*
> *Who remains standing when I die.*

The Unmonument is my memorial placed upside down in the earth. This least obtrusive of reminders will disturb no one, being in fact a way of burying my death. The inverse of such a tactic would be the unburial of my life. That is, so long as my monument is underground, my life shall remain above. Friend, you are my collaborator in this venture. How much pleasure it gives me to imagine you standing on the very ground that covers my statue, saying:

From south and east and west and north,
roads coming together have led me
to my secret center . . .

And of course it will be late in the day and you will consider the events of your life from the greatest to the most humble. Again words will come to you:

Now I can forget them. I reach my center . . .
my mirror.
Soon I shall know who I am.

19

Spare my bones the fire,
Let me lie entire,
Underground or in the air,
Whichever, I don't care.

Remember the story of my death? Well, I planned it this far in advance. And I did it for you, so you might understand it as none of the others could. When I leaned back on the cold pillows, staring through the open window at the black velvety sky, pointing, though my hand was on the verge of collapsing, and said in a clear, calm voice, "Look! Look!," I was asking the impossible of those loyal friends who were crowded into that small room. For they looked out the window and, seeing nothing, said almost in unison, "What is it?" And I replied in a tone that soothed and urged at once, "There! There!" In a moment I was dead. That is the famous story of my death told, I believe, for a dozen or so years and then forgotten. It is yours because you have found The Monument. Finding The Monument is what I urged when I said, "Look! Look!"

20

It is my belief that on a certain day in a person's life the shapes of all the clouds in the sky will for a single moment directly over his head resemble him. It has been the sad lot of almost everyone who has ever lived to miss this spectacle, but it has not been so with me. Today I saw The Monument affirmed in heaven. I sat in a chair and looked up by chance and this is what I saw.

A story is told of a man who lived his life anticipating his moment in the heavens, and each day there were clouds, he would lie on his back in front of his house. He did this summer and winter and the only rest he got was on clear days or days completely overcast. Finally, when he was very old, he did see himself in the clouds and died immediately after. They found him up on his platform, his eyes wide open, the look of astonishment still upon them.

21

We are truly ourselves only when we coincide with nothing, not even ourselves.

Where do I come from? Though unimportant and irrelevant to so single-minded a venture as The Monument, I believe if I included a few paragraphs from an abandoned autobiography you would see for yourself that I am justified in leaving my life out of our work.

> I have always said, when speaking of my father's father, Emil, that he died a sudden and tragic death by falling into a giant vat of molten metal. The fact is I know only what my father told me—that he suffered an accident in a steel mill and died. The terseness of my father's explanation (no doubt masking some pain at recalling this stage in his own life) created an impression of mystery and violence in my mind. Since the vat of molten metal was the only image I had of the inside of a steel mill, it actually became for me the sole cause of my grandfather's death. And the horror of it put him in a heroic perspective, a perspective which contributed to my impulse to aggrandize my father. As a small boy I wanted a lineage of heroes. It is significant that I would usually add, as epilogue to the tale of Emil's death, the suggestion that he was now part of a Cleveland skyscraper. There is some primitive irony in this, but also a belief in the ultimate utility of his dying, as though it were not merely an accident but self-sacrifice for the public good. His death has become over the years a myth of origin to which I cling almost unconsciously. I say "almost" because whenever I tell of it I am aware of the slight distortion I may be guilty of. Nevertheless, I feel a compulsion to tell it the way I originally construed it, regardless of the doubts that have increased over the years, and the young boy in me is satisfied.

> Of my father's mother, Ida, I have no image whatever, probably because my father had none either. She died giving birth to him. He weighed fifteen pounds.

22

. . . he ordered them to dig a grave at once, of the right size, and then collect any pieces of marble that they could find and fetch wood and water for the disposal of the corpse. As they bustled about obediently, he muttered through his tears: "Dead! And so great an artist!"

It is good none of my enemies, friends, or colleagues has seen this, for they would complain of my narcissism as they always seem to, but with—so they would claim—greater cause. They would mistake this modest document as self-centered in the extreme, not only because none of their names appears in it, but because I have omitted to mention my wife or daughter. How mistaken they are. This poor document does not have to do with a self, it dwells on the absence of a self. I—and this pronoun will have to do—have not permitted anything worthwhile or memorable to be part of this communication that strains even to exist in a language other than the one in which it was written. So much is excluded that it could not be a document of self-centeredness. If it is a mirror to anything, it is to the gap between the nothing that was and the nothing that will be. It is a thread of longing that binds past and future. Again, it is everything that history is not.

23

It is easy to lose oneself in nothing because nothing can interrupt and be unnoticed. Why do I do this?

24

There is a day when the daughters of Necessity sit on their thrones and chant and souls gather to choose the next life they will live.

After the despots pick beggary, and the beggars pick wealth, and Orpheus picks swanhood, Agamemnon an eagle, Ajax a lion, and Odysseus the life of quiet obscurity, I come along, pushing my way through the musical animals, and pick one of the lots. Since I had no need to compensate for any previous experience and wandered onto that meadow by chance, I found the lot of another man much like me, which is how I found you. And instead of going to the River of Unmindfulness, I wrote this down.

25

The most enclosed being generates waves.

Suppose the worst happens and I am still around while you are reading this? Suppose everybody is around? Well, there is the crystal box!

26

I confess a yearning to make prophetic remarks, to be remembered as someone who was ahead of his time; I would like to be someone about whom future generations would say, as they shifted from foot to foot and stared at the ground, "He knew! He knew!" But I don't know. I know only you, you ahead of my time. I know it is sad, even silly, this longing to say something that will charm or amaze others later on. But one little phrase is all I ask. Friend, say something amazing *for* me. It must be something you take for granted, something meaningless to you, but impossible for me to think of. Say I predicted it. Write it here:

[Translator's note: *Though I wanted to obey the author's request, I could not without violating what I took to be his desire for honesty. I believe he not only wanted it this way but might have predicted it.*]

27

I am so glad you discovered me. The treatment I have received is appalling. The army of angry poets coming out to whip The Monument.

28

I have begun to mistrust you, my dear friend, and I am sorry. As I proceed with this work, I sense your wish to make it your own. True, I have, in a way, given it to you, but it is precisely this spirit of "giving" that must be preserved. You must not "take" what is not really yours. No doubt I am being silly, my fears reflecting jealousy on my part, but I know you only as you work on this text. Whatever else you are is hidden from me. What I fear is that you will tell people in your day that you made up The Monument, that this is a mock translation, that I am merely a creature of your imagination. I know that I intend this somewhat, but the sweet anonymity and nothingness that I claim as my province *do* cause me pain. As I write, I feel that this should not be my memorial, merely, but that it should be passed on in no one's name, not even yours.

29

It occurs to me that you may be a woman. What then? I suppose I become therefore a woman. If you are a woman, I suggest that you curl up inside the belly of The Monument which is buried horizontally in the ground and eventually let yourself out through the mouth. Thus I can experience, however belatedly, a birth, your birth, the birth of myself as a woman.

30

... a Poet's mind
Is labour not unworthy of regard.

And what I say unto you, I say unto all, Watch!

Sometimes when I wander in these woods whose prince I am, I hear a voice and I know that I am not alone. Another voice, another monument becoming one; another tomb, another marker made from elements least visible; another voice that says *Watch it closely*. And I do, and there is someone inside. It is the Bishop, who after all was not intended to be seen. It is the Bishop calling and calling.

31

Such good work as yours should not go unrewarded, so I have written a speech for you, knowing how tired you must be. It should be delivered into the mirror.

Labors of hate! Labors of love! I can't go on working this way, shedding darkness, shucking light, peeling pages. There is no virtue in it. The author is the opposite of a good author, allowing no people in his work, allowing no plot to carry it forward. Where are the good phrases? They're borrowed! It all adds up to greed—his words in my mouth, his time in my time. He longs to be alive, to continue, yet he says he is nobody. Does he have nothing to say? Probably not. Anonymous, his eyes are fixed upon himself. I grow tired of his jabbering, the freight of his words. My greatest hope is his continued anonymity, which is why I bother to finish The Monument.

[Translator's note: *I must say that he has expressed my feeling so adequately that I find myself admiring him for it and hating myself somewhat.*]

32

Flotillas! Floating gardens skimming the sky's blue shell. Great gangs of gang-gangs and galahs. The air has never been so pure, my lungs are two pink sacks of moist down-under light. Friend, The Monument shines in the tabernacle of air, and at night, under the Southern Cross and the silent sparkling bed of stars, it sings. Friend, this is the place to do your monument. Go among the gang-gangs and galahs!

33

The drift of skeletons under the earth, the shifting of that dark society, those nations of the dead, the unshaping of their bones into dirt, the night of nothing removing them, turning their absences into the small zeros of the stars, it is indeed a grave, invisible workmanship. O Monument, what can be done!

34

They are back, the angry poets. But look! They have come with hammers and little buckets, and they are knocking off pieces of The Monument to study and use in the making of their own small tombs.

35

SONG OF MYSELF

First silence, then some humming,
then more silence, then nothing,
then more nothing, then silence,
then more silence, then nothing.

Song of My Other Self: There is no other self.

The Wind's Song: Get out of my way.

The Sky's Song: You're less than a cloud.

The Tree's Song: You're less than a leaf.

The Sea's Song: You're a wave, less than a wave.

The Sun's Song: You're the moon's child.

The Moon's Song: You're no child of mine.

36

There is a sullen, golden greed in my denials. Yet I wish I were not
merely making them up; I wish I could be the lies I tell. This is the
truth. Knowledge never helped me sort out anything, and having
had no knowledge but of nothing suggests all questions are unan-
swerable once they are posed. Asking is the act of unresolving, a
trope for disclosure.

37

. . . it is to be remembered that to raise a Monument is a sober and reflective act; that the inscription which it bears is intended to be permanent and for universal perusal; and that, for this reason, the thoughts and feelings expressed should be permanent also— liberated from that weakness and anguish of sorrow which is in nature transitory, and which with instinctive decency retires from notice. The passions should be subdued, the emotions controlled; strong indeed, but nothing ungovernable or wholly involuntary. Seemliness requires this, and truth requires it also: for how can the Narrator otherwise be trusted?

Julius Scaliger, who in a sleepless Fit of the Gout could make two hundred Verses in a Night, would have but five plain Words upon his Tomb.

Tell me that my ugly tomb, my transcending gesture, my way into the next world, your world, my world made by you, you the future of me, my future, my features translated, tell me that it will improve, that it will seem better for my not giving in to what passes for style, that its prose shall never wear a poem's guise at last, tell me that its perpetual prose will become less than itself and hint always at more.

38

The epic of disbelief
blares oftener and soon . . .

Some will think I wrote this and some will think you wrote this. The fact is neither of us did. There is a ghostly third who has taken up residence in this pen, this pen we hold. Not tangible enough to be described but easy to put a finger on, it is the text already written, unwriting itself into the text of promise. It blooms in its ashes, radiates health in its sickness. It is a new falsity, electric in its clumsiness, glad in its lies. And it loves itself as it fears death.

39

I wonder if my poverty would be more complete without you or whether you complete it, the last straw taken away. Having said such a thing, I feel a surge of power, I, a single strand, upright, making translation less and less possible. Beautiful swipes of clarity fall upon me, lights from the luminous bells of heaven. I tell you this robe of harmless flames I wear is no poor man's torn pajamas. There's no poverty here, with or without you. Translate. Translate faster. Brief work, isn't it, this feathery fluke!

40

To be the first of the posthumous poets is to be the oldest. This will make children of the poets of Europe, the dead poets of Europe. There must be something America is first in. Death and post-death meditations! Glory be! A crown on our heads at last! But what is America to you or you to America?

41

Solemn truths! Lucid inescapable foolishness! None of that for me! To be the salt of Walt, oceanic in osteality! Secure in cenotaph! The hysterical herald of hypogea! The fruit of the tomb! The flute of the tomb! The loot of gloom! The lute of loot! The work of soon, of never and ever! Saver of naught. Naughtiness of severance. Hoot of hiddenness. I give you my graven grave, my wordy ossuary, telltale trinket of transcendence, bauble of babble, tower of tripe, trap of tribute, thought-taxi from one day to the next, nougat of nothing, germ of gemini, humble hypogeum!

42

We have come to terms without terms, come round almost to the end. A relief, but only a stage, bare stage, first stage. We have allowed the enormous airs of the future to engulf us—to be sung, to be borne and born. Heirs of ourselves, ourselves heirs, salvos of air. Without weight the future is possible, here without our waiting. I embrace you in this madness, this muscular mouthing of possibles. The enormous airs—the giant cloudsongs that will reign and reign. Friend, they are coming and only we know it. Perhaps we should be silent, tell no one, and the airs will pass, pass without knowledge of themselves, never having been termed, tuned in turmoil, termed harmless.

43

Heavy glory upon us. Hang on. I must praise my brothers and sisters in the lost art, spitting into the wind, beating their heads against the stars, eating their words, putting their feet in their mouths, hating each other, all of them either lovely or fearful.

44

I feel nostalgia for poetry and believe The Monument should have some lines like:

Invisible lords among the stars
Over the heads of deep astronomers

or:

The moon sucking the sea, sucking
The light from our eyes as we sleep

That sort of thing. But it would never do. Too hard to translate out of the original. After the blazing plainness of The Monument's prose it doesn't stand up. And yet, there's a longing that has no voice and wants one, that fears it will die of itself. There are moments that crave memorial as if they were worthy, as if they were history and not merely in it, moments of the bluest sky, of the most intense sun, of the greatest happiness of the least known man or woman, moments that may have gone on for years in the most remote village on earth. They shall exist outside The Monument.

45

We are the enemies of pastoral violence, lovers of cold; the body recumbent like The Monument is for us the goodest good; heavy allusions to weather are just another load to us. Give us a good cigar, a long ash that we can speculate on. And plenty of smoke. Ho-hum. Now give us a glass of Spanish brandy. Give us a blank wall that we might see ourselves more truly and more strange. Now give us the paper, the daily paper on which to write. Now give us the day, this day. Take it away. The space that is left is The Monument.

46

It is the crystal box again. Let it be a sunlit tomb, a clear tumulus. Let us stand by it, by the life it promises. If we bask in its brightness, we shall be saved, we shall grow into the language that calls from the future, The Monument reaching out.

47

Spin out from your entrails, therefore, my soul, and let come what may! More empty space, more void . . .

Till the bridge you will need be form'd, till the ductile anchor hold, Till the gossamer thread you fling catch somewhere, O my soul.

Prose is the language of meaning so I suppose I mean what I say. I say what I say because it is prose. And so it is; describing the circle, the naught of my means, I am taking away, subtracting myself from my words. My blank prose travels into the future, its freight the fullness of zero, the circumference of absence. And it misses something, something I remember I wanted. Soon I shall disappear into the well of want, the lux of lack.

48

It is the giant of nothingness that rises beyond, that rises beyond beyondness, undiscovered in the vault of the future, in the leap of faith. If there were a limb here, a limb there, on the desert sand, *that* would be something. If on the pedestal these words appeared: "I am The Monument. Should you doubt this, look around you and compare," *that* would be something. But The Monument has no monument. There are no powers that will work for it; earth, sky, and breathing of the common air, all will forget. O most unhappy Monument! The giant of nothingness rising in sleep like the beginning of language, like language being born into the sleeper's future, his dream of himself entering the beyond. O happy Monument! The giant of nothing is taking you with him!

49

I have no apologies, no words for disbelievers. What do I care if there is nothing sublime in this summery encounter with the void or voided mirror? We go our ways, each without the other, going without a theory of direction, going because we have to. Why make excuses? Friend, tell them I see myself only as happy. Let them say what they will, The Monument will pretend to be dead.

50

Here I lie dead, and here I wait for thee:
So thou shalt wait
Soon for some other; since all mortals be
Bound to one fate.

Our Fathers finde their graves in our short memories, and sadly tell us how we may be buried in our Survivors.

Now here I am at the end waiting for you, ahead of my time, ahead of yours. Such irony should be its own reward, but here I am at the end, the letter ended, The Monument concluded, but only briefly; for it must continue, must gather its words and send them off into another future, your future, my future. O poor Monument to offer so little even to those who have made you!

51

If I were to die now without The Monument, none of my words would remain. How sad it is to think of the hours wasted while this triumph of ease and crudity that has taken so little time should last centuries, towering over the corpses of poems whose lyrical natures flew off like the best intentions. If I were to die now, I would change my name so it might appear that the author of my works were still alive. No I wouldn't. If I were to die now, it would be only a joke, a cruel joke played on fortune. If I were to die now, your greatest work would remain forever undone. My last words would be, "Don't finish it."

52

. . . Oh, how do I bear to go on living! And how could I bear to die now!

O living always, always dying!
O the burials of me past and present,
O me while I stride ahead, material, visible, imperious as ever;
O me, what I was for years, now dead, (I lament not, I am content;)
O to disengage myself from those corpses of me, which I turn and look
    at where I cast them,
To pass on, (O living! always living!) and leave the corpses behind.

from *SELECTED POEMS*

SHOOTING WHALES

for Judith and Leon Major

When the shoals of plankton
swarmed into St. Margaret's Bay,
turning the beaches pink,
we saw from our place on the hill
the sperm whales feeding,
fouling the nets
in their play,
and breaching clean
so the humps of their backs
rose over the wide sea meadows.

Day after day
we waited inside
for the rotting plankton to disappear.
The smell stilled even the wind,
and the oxen looked stunned,
pulling hay on the slope
of our hill.
But the plankton kept coming in
and the whales would not go.

That's when the shooting began.
The fishermen got in their boats
and went after the whales,
and my father and uncle
and we children went, too.
The froth of our wake sank fast
in the wind-shaken water.

The whales surfaced close by.
Their foreheads were huge,
the doors of their faces were closed.
Before sounding, they lifted
their flukes into the air
and brought them down hard.
They beat the sea into foam,
and the path that they made
shone after them.

Though I did not see their eyes,
I imagined they were
like the eyes of mourning,
glazed with rheum,
watching us, sweeping along
under the darkening sheets of salt.

When we cut our engine and waited
for the whales to surface again,
the sun was setting,
turning the rock-strewn barrens a gaudy salmon.
A cold wind flailed at our skin.
When finally the sun went down
and it seemed like the whales had gone,
my uncle, no longer afraid,
shot aimlessly into the sky.

Three miles out
in the rolling dark
under the moon's astonished eyes,
our engine would not start
and we headed home in the dinghy.
And my father, hunched over the oars,
brought us in. I watched him,
rapt in his effort, rowing against the tide,
his blond hair glistening with salt.
I saw the slick spillage of moonlight
being blown over his shoulders,
and the sea and spindrift
suddenly silver.

He did not speak the entire way.

At midnight
when I went to bed,
I imagined the whales
moving beneath me,
sliding over the weed-covered hills of the deep;
they knew where I was;
they were luring me
downward and downward
into the murmurous
waters of sleep.

NIGHTS IN HACKETT'S COVE

Those nights lit by the moon and the moon's nimbus,
the bones of the wrecked pier rose crooked in air
and the sea wore a tarnished coat of silver.
The black pines waited. The cold air smelled
of fishheads rotting under the pier at low tide.
The moon kept shedding its silver clothes
over the bogs and pockets of bracken.
Those nights I would gaze at the bay road,
at the cottages clustered under the moon's immaculate stare,
nothing hinted that I would suffer so late
this turning away, this longing to be there.

A MORNING

I have carried it with me each day: that morning I took
my uncle's boat from the brown water cove
and headed for Mosher Island.
Small waves splashed against the hull
and the hollow creak of oarlock and oar
rose into the woods of black pine crusted with lichen.
I moved like a dark star, drifting over the drowned
other half of the world until, by a distant prompting,
I looked over the gunwale and saw beneath the surface
a luminous room, a light-filled grave, saw for the first time
the one clear place given to us when we are alone.

MY MOTHER ON AN EVENING IN LATE SUMMER

1

When the moon appears
and a few wind-stricken barns stand out
in the low-domed hills
and shine with a light
that is veiled and dust-filled
and that floats upon the fields,
my mother, with her hair in a bun,
her face in shadow, and the smoke
from her cigarette coiling close
to the faint yellow sheen of her dress,
stands near the house
and watches the seepage of late light
down through the sedges,
the last gray islands of cloud
taken from view, and the wind
ruffling the moon's ash-colored coat
on the black bay.

2

Soon the house, with its shades drawn closed, will send
small carpets of lampglow
into the haze and the bay
will begin its loud heaving
and the pines, frayed finials
climbing the hill, will seem to graze
the dim cinders of heaven.
And my mother will stare into the starlanes,
the endless tunnels of nothing,

and as she gazes,
under the hour's spell,
she will think how we yield each night
to the soundless storms of decay
that tear at the folding flesh,
and she will not know
why she is here
or what she is prisoner of
if not the conditions of love that brought her to this.

3

My mother will go indoors
and the fields, the bare stones
will drift in peace, small creatures—
the mouse and the swift—will sleep
at opposite ends of the house.
Only the cricket will be up,
repeating its one shrill note
to the rotten boards of the porch,
to the rusted screens, to the air, to the rimless dark,
to the sea that keeps to itself.
Why should my mother awake?
The earth is not yet a garden
about to be turned. The stars
are not yet bells that ring
at night for the lost.
It is much too late.

LEOPARDI

The night is warm and clear and without wind.
The stone-white moon waits above the rooftops
and above the nearby river. Every street is still
and the corner lights shine down only upon the hunched shapes of cars.
You are asleep. And sleep gathers in your room
and nothing at this moment bothers you. Jules,
an old wound has opened and I feel the pain of it again.
While you sleep I have gone outside to pay my late respects
to the sky that seems so gentle
and to the world that is not and that says to me:
"I do not give you any hope. Not even hope."
Down the street there is the voice of a drunk
singing an unrecognizable song
and a car a few blocks off.
Things pass and leave no trace,
and tomorrow will come and the day after,
and whatever our ancestors knew time has taken away.
They are gone and their children are gone
and the great nations are gone.
And the armies are gone that sent clouds of dust and smoke
rolling across Europe. The world is still and we do not hear them.
Once when I was a boy, and the birthday I had waited for
was over, I lay on my bed, awake and miserable, and very late
that night the sound of someone's voice singing down a side street,
dying little by little into the distance,
wounded me, as this does now.

THE CONTINUOUS LIFE

THE IDEA

for Nolan Miller

For us, too, there was a wish to possess
Something beyond the world we knew, beyond ourselves,
Beyond our power to imagine, something nevertheless
In which we might see ourselves; and this desire
Came always in passing, in waning light, and in such cold
That ice on the valley's lakes cracked and rolled,
And blowing snow covered what earth we saw,
And scenes from the past, when they surfaced again,
Looked not as they had, but ghostly and white
Among false curves and hidden erasures;
And never once did we feel we were close
Until the night wind said, "Why do this,
Especially now? Go back to the place you belong";
And there appeared, with its windows glowing, small,
In the distance, in the frozen reaches, a cabin;
And we stood before it, amazed at its being there,
And would have gone forward and opened the door,
And stepped into the glow and warmed ourselves there,
But that it was ours by not being ours,
And should remain empty. That was the idea.

VELOCITY MEADOWS

I can say now that nothing was possible
But leaving the house and standing in front of it, staring
As long as I could into the valley. I knew that a train,
Trailing a scarf of smoke, would arrive, that soon it would rain.
A frieze of clouds lowered a shadow over the town,
And a driving wind flattened the meadows that swept
Beyond the olive trees and banks of hollyhock and rose.
The air smelled sweet, and a girl was waving a stick
At some crows so far away they seemed like flies.
Her mother, wearing a cape and shawl, shielded her eyes.
I wondered from what, since there was no sun. Then someone
Appeared and said, "Look at those clouds forming a wall, those crows
Falling out of the sky, those fields, pale green, green-yellow,
Rolling away, and that girl and her mother, waving goodbye."
In a moment the sky was stained with a reddish haze,
And the person beside me was running away. It was dusk,
The lights of the town were coming on, and I saw, dimly at first,
Close to the graveyard bound by rows of cypress bending down,
The girl and her mother, next to each other,
Smoking, grinding their heels into the ground.

A.M.

for Lee Rust Brown

. . . And here the dark infinitive to feel,
Which would endure and have the earth be still
And the star-strewn night pour down the mountains
Into the hissing fields and silent towns until the last
Insomniac turned in, must end, and early risers see
The scarlet clouds break up and golden plumes of smoke
From uniform dark homes turn white, and so on down
To the smallest blade of grass and fallen leaf
Touched by the arriving light. Another day has come,
Another fabulous escape from the damages of night,
So even the gulls, in the ragged circle of their flight,
Above the sea's long lanes that flash and fall, scream
Their approval. How well the sun's rays probe
The rotting carcass of a skate, how well
They show the worms and swarming flies at work,
How well they shine upon the fatal sprawl
Of everything on earth. How well they love us all.

CENTO VIRGILIANUS

And so, passing under the dome of the great sky,
Driven by storms and heavy seas, we came,
Wondering on what shore of the world
We were cast up. The howling of dogs
Was heard across the twilight,
And over the tombs the rumbling sound
A grassfire makes when it is whipped by the wind;
And later on, from icy courtyards,
The high-pitched wails of women rose
Against the silent golden stars.
At first, we didn't miss the towns we'd started from—
The houses painted pink and green, the swans feeding
Among the river reeds, the showers of summer light
Sweeping over the pasturelands.
So what if we'd hoped to find Apollo here,
Enthroned at last, so what if a cramping cold
Chilled us to the bone. We'd come to a place
Where everything weeps for how the world goes.

ORPHEUS ALONE

It was an adventure much could be made of: a walk
On the shores of the darkest known river,
Among the hooded, shoving crowds, by steaming rocks
And rows of ruined huts half-buried in the muck;
Then to the great court with its marble yard
Whose emptiness gave him the creeps, and to sit there
In the sunken silence of the place and speak
Of what he had lost, what he still possessed of his loss,
And, then, pulling out all the stops, describing her eyes,
Her forehead where the golden light of evening spread,
The curve of her neck, the slope of her shoulders, everything
Down to her thighs and calves, letting the words come,
As if lifted from sleep, to drift upstream,
Against the water's will, where all the condemned
And pointless labor, stunned by his voice's cadence,
Would come to a halt, and even the crazed, disheveled
Furies, for the first time, would weep, and the soot-filled
Air would clear just enough for her, the lost bride,
To step through the image of herself and be seen in the light.
As everyone knows, this was the first great poem,
Which was followed by days of sitting around
In the houses of friends, with his head back, his eyes
Closed, trying to will her return, but finding
Only himself, again and again, trapped
In the chill of his loss, and, finally,
Without a word, taking off to wander the hills
Outside of town, where he stayed until he had shaken
The image of love and put in its place the world

As he wished it would be, urging its shape and measure
Into speech of such newness that the world was swayed,
And trees suddenly appeared in the bare place
Where he spoke and lifted their limbs and swept
The tender grass with the gowns of their shade,
And stones, weightless for once, came and set themselves there,
And small animals lay in the miraculous fields of grain
And aisles of corn, and slept. The voice of light
Had come forth from the body of fire, and each thing
Rose from its depths and shone as it never had.
And that was the second great poem,
Which no one recalls anymore. The third and greatest
Came into the world as the world, out of the unsayable,
Invisible source of all longing to be; it came
As things come that will perish, to be seen or heard
Awhile, like the coating of frost or the movement
Of wind, and then no more; it came in the middle of sleep
Like a door to the infinite, and, circled by flame,
Came again at the moment of waking, and, sometimes,
Remote and small, it came as a vision with trees
By a weaving stream, brushing the bank
With their violet shade, with somebody's limbs
Scattered among the matted, mildewed leaves nearby,
With his severed head rolling under the waves,
Breaking the shifting columns of light into a swirl
Of slivers and flecks; it came in a language
Untouched by pity, in lines, lavish and dark,
Where death is reborn and sent into the world as a gift,
So the future, with no voice of its own, nor hope
Of ever becoming more than it will be, might mourn.

FEAR OF THE NIGHT

ALCETUS: I'm telling you, Melissus,
      Looking at the moon just now
      Reminds me of a dream I had last night.
      I stood at the window, looking at the sky,
      And suddenly the moon began to fall.
      It came straight at me, getting nearer
      And nearer until it crashed
      Like a bowl beside the house.
      Then it burst into flame, then fizzled
      Like a hot coal dropped in water.
      It turned black, and the grass was singed.
      And that was the way the moon went out.
      But there was more to it than that.
      When I looked up, I saw an opening in the dark.
      It was the hole from which the moon
      Had rolled down out of the sky.
      I'm telling you, Melissus,
      I was scared and still am.

MELISSUS: And why shouldn't you be?
      After all, the moon *could* fall at any time.

ALCETUS: That's right, look at the stars,
      They fall all summer long.

MELISSUS: But there are lots of stars,
And if a few of them fall, so what?
There are thousands left.
But there is only one moon in the sky
And no one has seen it fall but in dreams.

(AFTER LEOPARDI)

TWO LETTERS

1 GRETE SAMSA'S LETTER TO H.

Dear H., we have been in the new house almost a year, and mother and father have recovered from their ordeal. It is hard to imagine how painful it was for them. As for me, I sleep late as always and practice the violin. But to answer your questions about Gregor: Yes, I admit I am still troubled by what happened to him. Not that I am confident any of us wakes up the same as we were upon falling asleep. Only the most foolish of us believes we don't change. But who would have thought of going so far! Was Gregor enacting the first stage of a terrible privacy? The last stage of a disfiguring illness? Was he preparing for death in a new and spectacular way? Or was he trying to prove that without inhibitions we become not Berninis or Raphaels but what he became? Perhaps what happened is best seen as a form of religious protest with Gregor allegorizing our hopeless term on earth, except that his interest in spiritual matters could hardly be said to exist. Poor boy! He was after all a poet who, in deference to others, kept his calling a secret. Might we consider his hideous change, then, an indiscretion, a kind of counterlife, a fictive existence in which he became his work? Whatever the case, there were moments when Gregor, already bronzed by the instreaming light of his window, appeared a miraculous monument to himself, both smaller and larger than life. He probably thought that the world, despite its cities, had not begun in earnest, so why not fool around. Alas, I myself have started to feel the onset of something, a sadness perhaps, the dawn of a new season, an existence even. But enough of this. Tell me about yourself and what it is like where you are. Do the leaves ever stop falling? Are the shadows ever anything but long? And the mountains? Can one see them?

Dear H., this interest in me, in what I was for a limited time, is upsetting. I have divined the content of my sister's letter from a privileged perspective, and am astonished that even you should be puzzled by what happened to me. Do we not, if we are lucky, live many lives, assume many masks, and, with death always imminent, do we not keep hoping to be reborn? This is the human condition. We are citizens of one world only when we apply to the next; we are perpetual exiles, living on the outside of what is possible, creating for ourselves the terms of our exclusion, yet hoping to overcome them. Our misery and our happiness are inextricable. So I ask you, why so much attention given to just one life? What of my other lives? Not that I wish to play down my life as an insect. Why should I? It was my strength, my necessity, my triumph. I became what my colleague Raban only toyed with becoming. I gave those who knew me the chance to believe in something that appeared to contradict truth. And yet, I was real, as real as anything. I was irreducible, original, the source of a beautiful and belligerent antinomianism. No amount of disbelief could undo me—undo me into what? My absence? So I could be missed, and thus more present? Oh my dear H., the injustice of life! My best days have been taken from me. I speak to you now from the other side, from yet another exile, changed into a man without meaning or message, living in southern California, getting by as well as I can. How I long for the past, its blend of confusion and terror, its stretches of solitude. To be back in my old room, my old bed, how perfect that seems to me now—now that I feel once more the unknown staring down at the known as if hoping to be recognized into existence. I am speaking, of course, of the work before me. What sadness, what joy.

CHEKHOV: A SESTINA

Why him? He woke up and felt anxious. He was out of sorts, out of character. If only it would go away. Ivashin loved Nadya Vishnyevskaya and was afraid of his love. When the butler told him the old lady had just gone out, but that the young lady was at home, he fumbled in his fur coat and dress coat pocket, found his card, and said: "Right." But it was not right. Driving from his house in the morning to pay a visit, he thought he was compelled to it by the conventions of society which weighed heavily upon him. But now it was clear that he went to pay calls only because somewhere far away in the depths of his soul, as under a veil, there lay hidden a hope that he would see Nadya, his secret love. And he suddenly felt pitiful, sad, and not a little anxious. In his soul, it seemed to him, it was snowing, and everything was fading away. He was afraid to love Nadya, because he thought he was too old for her, his appearance unattractive, and did not believe that a young woman like her could love a man for his mind or spiritual character. Everything was dim, sharing, he felt, the same blank character. Still, there would rise at times in him something like hope, a glimpse of happiness, of things turning out all right. Then, just as quickly, it would pass away. And he would wonder what had come over him. Why should he, a retired councillor of state, educated, liberal-minded, a well-traveled man, why should he, in other words, be so anxious? Were there not other women with whom he could fall in love? Surely, it was always possible to fall in love. It was possible, moreover, to fall in love without acting out of character. There was absolutely no need for him to be anxious. To be in love, to have a young pretty wife and children of his own, was not a crime or a deception, but his right. Clearly, there was something wrong with him. He wished he were far away . . . But suddenly he heard from somewhere in the house the young officer's spurs jingle and then die away. That instant marked the death of his timid love. And in its vanishing, he felt the seeds of a different sort of melancholy take root within him. Whatever happened now, whatever desolation might be his, it would build character. Yes, he thought, so it is only right. Yes, all is finished, and I'm glad, very glad, yes, and I'm not let down, no, nor am I in any way anxious. No, certainly not anxious. What he had to do now was to get away. But how could he make it look right? How could he have thought he was in love? How out of character! How very unlike him!

TO HIMSELF

So you've come to me now without knowing why;
Nor why you sit in the ruby plush of an ugly chair, the sly
Revealing angle of light turning your hair a silver gray;
Nor why you have chosen this moment to set the writing of years
Against the writing of nothing; you who narrowed your eyes,
Peering into the polished air of the hallway mirror, and said
You were mine, all mine; who begged me to write, but always
Of course to you, without ever saying what it was for;
Who used to whisper in my ear only the things
You wanted to hear; who come to me now and say
That it's late, that the trees are bending under the wind,
That night will fall; as if there were something
You wanted to know, but for years had forgotten to ask,
Something to do with sunlight slanting over a table,
An arm rising, a face turning, and far
In the distance a car disappearing over the hill.

FICTION

I think of the innocent lives
Of people in novels who know they'll die
But not that the novel will end. How different they are
From us. Here, the moon stares dumbly down,
Through scattered clouds, onto the sleeping town,
And the wind rounds up the fallen leaves,
And somebody—namely me—deep in his chair,
Riffles the pages left, knowing there's not
Much time for the man and woman in the rented room,
For the red light over the door, for the iris
Tossing its shadow against the wall; not much time
For the soldiers under the trees that line
The river, for the wounded being hauled away
To the cities of the interior where they will stay;
The war that raged for years will come to a close,
And so will everything else, except for a presence
Hard to define, a trace, like the scent of grass
After a night of rain or the remains of a voice
That lets us know without spelling it out
Not to despair; if the end is come, it too will pass.

LUMINISM

And though it was brief, and slight, and nothing
To have been held on to so long, I remember it,
As if it had come from within, one of the scenes
The mind sets for itself, night after night, only
To part from, quickly and without warning. Sunlight
Flooded the valley floor and blazed on the town's
Westward-facing windows. The streets shimmered like rivers,
And trees, bushes, and clouds were caught in the spill,
And nothing was spared, not the couch we sat on,
Nor the rugs, nor our friends, staring off into space.
Everything drowned in the golden fire. Then Philip
Put down his glass and said: "This hand is just one
In an infinite series of hands. Imagine."
And that was it. The evening dimmed and darkened
Until the western rim of the sky took on
The purple look of a bruise, and everyone stood
And said what a great sunset it had been. This was a while ago,
And it was remarkable, but something else happened then—
A cry, almost beyond our hearing, rose and rose,
As if across time, to touch us as nothing else would,
And so lightly we might live out our lives and not know.
I had no idea what it meant until now.

LIFE IN THE VALLEY

Like many brilliant notions—easy to understand
But hard to believe—the one about our hating it here
Was put aside and then forgot. Those freakish winds
Over the flaming lake, bearing down, bringing a bright
Electrical dust, an ashen air crowded with leaves—
Fallen, ghostly—shading the valley, filling it with
A rushing sound, were not enough to drive us out.
Nor were those times the faded winter sun
Lowered a frozen half-light over the canyons
And silent storms buried the high resorts
With heavy snows. We simply stayed indoors.
Our friends would say the views—starlight over
The clustered domes and towers, the frigid moon
In the water's glass—were great. And we agreed,
And got to like the sight of iron horses rusting
In the fields, and birds with wings outspread,
Their silver bones glowing at the water's edge,
And far away, huge banks of cloud motionless as lead.

THE CONTINUOUS LIFE

What of the neighborhood homes awash
In a silver light, of children crouched in the bushes,
Watching the grown-ups for signs of surrender,
Signs that the irregular pleasures of moving
From day to day, of being adrift on the swell of duty,
Have run their course? Oh parents, confess
To your little ones the night is a long way off
And your taste for the mundane grows; tell them
Your worship of household chores has barely begun;
Describe the beauty of shovels and rakes, brooms and mops;
Say there will always be cooking and cleaning to do,
That one thing leads to another, which leads to another;
Explain that you live between two great darks, the first
With an ending, the second without one, that the luckiest
Thing is having been born, that you live in a blur
Of hours and days, months and years, and believe
It has meaning, despite the occasional fear
You are slipping away with nothing completed, nothing
To prove you existed. Tell the children to come inside,
That your search goes on for something you lost—a name,
A family album that fell from its own small matter
Into another, a piece of the dark that might have been yours,
You don't really know. Say that each of you tries
To keep busy, learning to lean down close and hear
The careless breathing of earth and feel its available
Languor come over you, wave after wave, sending
Small tremors of love through your brief,
Undeniable selves, into your days, and beyond.

FROM A LOST DIARY

I had not begun the great journey I was to undertake. I did not feel like it. At breakfast, I thought of writing to Goethe, but of course did not. I had not met him yet, so could not pretend to be on good terms with him. Would I sit for Raeburn? I turned it over a few times and chose not to. Why should I commit my looks on a particular day to the casual glances of history? I stared a long time at the green fields to the west of the house, and watched with numb fascination the immobility of two spotted cows. Lunch was out of the question, and so was the letter to Wordsworth. I was sure he would not respond. Would I myself write a poem? I had never written one, but decided that nothing would be lost by postponing the experiment. There is so much not to do! Not to visit Blake or Crabb Robinson. Not to write Corot and tell him about the cows. Not to write Turner about my vision of the sun that like a red cry sank and smothered in rippling water until finally far away the water fell into the soundless chasms of an infinite night. What a relief! My mother, hunched over her needlework, urged me to write my sister to whom I had nothing to say. "In many instances it is better and kinder to write nothing than not to write," said she, quoting someone or other. A day so much like the others, why do anything about it? Why even write this down, were it not for my going on record as not having lived. After all, who can believe what is not written down? That I have withdrawn from the abuses of time means little or nothing. I am a place, a place where things come together, then fly apart. Look at the fields disappearing, look at the distant hills, look at the night, the velvety, fragrant night, which has already come, though the sun continues to stand at my door.

TRAVEL

It might have been just outside Munich or Rome or on the new road between Santos and São Paulo. It might have been in New York right after the war or in Budapest or Sydney, and now Miami comes to mind. I was always traveling. When she kissed me, when she took off her clothes and begged me to take off mine, we might have been in Prague. When the wind broke tree limbs and shattered windowpanes, we were in Stockholm or almost there. So many places to keep track of. So many sights. It might have been in Philly. I don't know. I can't recall her name, but she sat next to me and put her hand in my pocket, just slipped it in. Later she told me she never spent a night alone, so we climbed into bed and she kept falling asleep. I kept my eyes on the moon. But what I'm talking about happened before Philly, during the dark days when I would lose track of what happened after breakfast. The rain was so heavy, I never opened the blinds. There was nothing to remind me of where I was. I'm not sure, but it might have been in London. She held my hand, then took off her clothes and posed before me, turning this way and that. I think she mentioned Bermuda. I think it was there that she wrapped her legs around me, there in that small room by the sea. I can't be sure. So much has happened. So many days have lost their luster. The miles I've gone keep unraveling. The air is tinged with mist. The cliffs must be closer than they look. I can't be sure. None of the old merriment is here, none of the flash and vigor, none of the pain that kept sending me elsewhere.

NARRATIVE POETRY

Yesterday at the supermarket I overheard a man and a woman discussing narrative poetry. She said: "Perhaps all so-called narrative poems are merely ironic, their events only pointing out how impoverished we are, how, like hopeless utopians, we live for the end. They show that our lives are invalidated by our needs, especially the need to continue. I've come to believe that narrative is born of self-hatred."

He said: "What concerns me is the narrative that provides no coherent framework for measuring temporal or spatial passage, the narrative in which the hero travels, believing he goes forward when in fact he stands still. He becomes the single connective, the embodiment of narrative, its terrible delusion, the nightmare of its own unreality."

I wanted to remind them that the narrative poem takes the place of an absent narrative and is always absorbing the other's absence so it can be named, and, at the same time, relinquishing its own presence to the awful solitudes of forgetfulness. The absent narrative is the one, I wanted to say, in which our fate is written. But they had gone before I could speak.

When I got home, my sister was sitting in the living room, waiting for me. I said to her: "You know, Sis, it just occurred to me that some narrative poems move so quickly they cannot be kept up with, and their progress must be imagined. They are the most lifelike and least real."

"Yes," said my sister. "But has it occurred to you that some narrative poems move so slowly we are constantly leaping ahead of them, imagining what they might be? And has it occurred to you that these are written most often in youth?"

Later I remembered the summer in Rome when I became convinced that narratives in which memory plays a part are self-defeating. It was hot, and I realized that memory is a memorial to events that could not sustain themselves into the present, which is why memory is tinged with pity and its music is always a dirge.

Then the phone rang. It was my mother calling to ask what I was doing. I told her I was working on a negative narrative, one that refuses to begin because beginning is meaningless in an infinite universe, and refuses to end for the same reason. It is all a suppressed middle, an unutterable and inexhaustible conjunction. "And, Mom," I said, "it is like the narrative that refuses to mask the essential and universal stillness, and so confines its remarks to what never happens."

Then my mother said: "Your dad used to talk to me about narrative poetry. He said it was a woman in a long gown who carried flowers. Her hair was red and fell lightly over her shoulders. He said narrative poetry happened usually in spring and involved a man. The woman would approach her house, wave to the man, and drop her flowers. This," Mom continued, "seemed a sign of narrative poetry's pointlessness. Wherever the woman was, she sowed seeds of disinterest."

"Mom," I ventured, "what we call narrative is simply submission to the predicate's insufferable claims on the future; it furthers continuance, blooms into another predicate. Don't you think that notions of closure rest on our longing for a barren predicate!"

"You're absolutely right," said my mother. "There's no other way to think of it." And she hung up.

ALWAYS

for Charles Simic

Always so late in the day
In their rumpled clothes, sitting
Around a table lit by a single bulb,
The great forgetters were hard at work.
They tilted their heads to one side, closing their eyes.
Then a house disappeared, and a man in his yard
With all his flowers in a row.
The great forgetters wrinkled their brows.
Then Florida went and San Francisco
Where tugs and barges leave
Small gleaming scars across the bay.
One of the great forgetters struck a match.
Gone were the harps of beaded lights
That vault the rivers of New York.
Another filled his glass
And that was it for crowds at evening
Under sulfur-yellow streetlamps coming on.
And afterward Bulgaria was gone, and then Japan.
"Where will it stop?" one of them said.
"Such difficult work, pursuing the fate
Of everything known," said another.
"Down to the last stone," said a third,
"And only the cold zero of perfection
Left for the imagination." And gone
Were North and South America,
And gone as well the moon.
One of the great forgetters coughed,
Another yawned, another gazed at the window:
No grass, no trees . . .
The blaze of promise everywhere.

GROTESQUES

1 THE HUNCHBACK

It was the middle of the night.
The beauty parlors were closed and the pale moon
    Raced above the water towers.
"Franz," screamed the woman, "take the corpse outside;
    It's impossible to think in here."
"Yes, ma'am," said the hunchback. When she was alone
    She undid the top two buttons
Of her blouse, crossed the room and played
    The upright in the corner there.
The brief arrangements of her feeling—flawless—
    Bloomed in the October chill.
Cold roses filled the rooms upstairs. Franz,
    Who stood beside the corpse, closed
His eyes and breathed the scented air. If only
    He could have such pleasure every night,
If only the amazing speech of love were not
    So frail and could be caught and held
Forever. Poor Franz. Time was always
    Spinning out of reach. The dark
Trees swayed above the bending blades of grass.
    A neighbor's dog, across whose back
Small dots of shadow strayed, had come to sniff
    The dead man's matted hair. Far off,
A caterwauling train whizzed past. Franz
    Stared for a moment at the dog,
Then quickly checked his watch. It was getting late.
    The wind was dying down. Then
The music stopped and the lights inside the house
    Went out. There was an anxious stillness

Everywhere. Franz turned to go. "Come back,"
　　The woman called. "I'm ready now."
But what about poor Franz? He wouldn't dare
　　Go back. An hour later, the woman
In a faded robe sat in the kitchen, playing
　　Solitaire, and Franz lay down
Beside the corpse and slept, unloved, untouched,
　　In the dull, moon-flooded garden air.

2 THE KING

Not far from the palace
The air was filled with haze
That swept, unhindered, into every open place,
And the sea like a blue quilt
Swelled and came apart.
Its blistered scrolls of stuffing littered the shore.
The king was pleased. "Great passions
Seek release," he thought.
Up the road, over the tawny seaside barrens
The sound of a flute caught his ear.
An old hotel, surrounded by arcades
And flanked by towers, lay just ahead.
The water in the swimming pool was clear
And marble gods and goddesses stood around.
Beyond an avenue of trees, half-open books
Were scattered on the lawn for visitors who liked to read.
The king bent down and read a page,
And praised the author, and wiped away a tear.
Farther on, packs of dogs waded in the waves
Of rising heat, or drowsed in the momentary shade
Of a passing cloud. Leafy trees hemmed in
Small tracts of all-white bungalows.
Shafts of heavy sunlight struck the ground.
Beside a house, next to a wood, a woman
In a bathing suit was hanging up her wash.
The king took off his crown and went to her.
Later, climbing from the bed, he thought,
"Have all my royal moments come to this?"
He patted her behind and motored off.
Two men were fishing from a boat, two others
Watching from the shore. The stillness

Of the scene filled him with remorse.
Was it craving for the unknown
That drove him over the countryside?
If a genius finds his subjects far from home,
Why shouldn't a king? He parked the car.
Under the fuss of starlight, under the dusty
Sickle of the moon, he stood alone,
And waited for the birds to sing,
For the wordless tirades of the wind.
He closed his eyes. There was nothing
In the ruins of the night that was not his.

3 THE COUPLE

The scene is a midtown station.
  The time is 3 a.m.
Jane is alone on the platform,
  Humming a requiem.

She leans against the tiles.
  She rummages in her purse
For something to ease a headache
  That just keeps getting worse.

She went to a boring party,
  And left without her date.
Now she's alone on the platform,
  And the trains are running late.

The subway station is empty,
  Seedy, sinister, gray.
Enter a well-dressed man
  Slowly heading Jane's way.

The man comes up beside her:
  "Excuse me, my name is John.
I hope I haven't disturbed you.
  If I have, then I'll be gone.

"I had a dream last night
  That I would meet somebody new.
After twenty-four hours of waiting,
  I'm glad she turned out to be you."

Oh where are the winds of morning?
    Oh where is love at first sight?
A man comes out of nowhere.
    Maybe he's Mr. Right.

How does one find the answer,
    If one has waited so long?
A man comes out of nowhere,
    He's probably Mr. Wrong.

Jane imagines the future,
    And almost loses heart.
She sees herself as Europe
    And John as Bonaparte.

They walk to the end of the platform.
    They stumble down to the tracks.
They stand among the wrappers
    And empty cigarette packs.

The wind blows through the tunnel.
    They listen to the sound.
The way it growls and whistles
    Holds them both spellbound.

Jane stares into the dark:
    "It's a wonder sex can be good
When most of the time it comes down to
    Whether one shouldn't or should."

John looks down at his watch:
   "I couldn't agree with you more,
And often it raises the question—
   'What are you saving it for?'"

They kneel beside each other
   As if they were in a trance,
Then Jane lifts up her dress
   And John pulls down his pants.

Everyone knows what happens,
   Or what two people do
When one is on top of the other
   Making a great to-do.

The wind blows through the tunnel
   Trying to find the sky.
Jane is breathing her hardest,
   And John begins to sigh:

"I'm a Princeton professor.
   God knows what drove me to this.
I have a wife and family;
   I've known marital bliss.

"But things were turning humdrum,
   And I felt I was being false.
Every night in our bedroom
   I wished I were someplace else."

What is the weather outside?
What is the weather within
That drives these two to excess
And into the arms of sin?

They are the children of Eros.
They move, but not too fast.
They want to extend their pleasure,
They want the moment to last.

Too bad they cannot hear us.
Too bad we can't advise.
Fate that brought them together
Has yet another surprise.

Just as they reach the utmost
Peak of their endeavor,
An empty downtown local
Separates them forever.

An empty downtown local
Screams through the grimy air
A couple dies in the subway;
Couples die everywhere.

SE LA VITA E SVENTURA . . . ?

for Charles Wright

Where was it written that today
I would go to the window and, because it was summer,
Imagine warm air filling the high floating rooms of trees
With the odors of grass and tar, that two crazed bees
Would chase each other around in the shade, that a wall
Of storm clouds would rise in the east,
That today of all days a man out walking would catch his breath
And lean his head back, letting the gilded light
Slide over his upturned face, and that a stranger
Appearing from nowhere, suddenly baring a knife,
Would rip him open from belly to sternum, making his moment
In front of my house his last? Where was it written
That the world, because it was merciful after all, would part
To make room for the blurred shape of the murderer
Fleeing the scene, while the victim, who had already
Slipped to his knees, would feel the heat of his whole being pass
Into a brief, translucent cloud unraveling as it was formed?
Or that a sightless gaze would replace his look of amazement,
That, despite what I guessed was his will to survive, to enter
Once more the unreachable sphere of light, he would continue
To fall, and the neighbors, who had gathered by now,
Would peer into his body's dark and watch him sinking
Into his wound like a fly or a mote, becoming
An infinitesimal part of the night, where the drift
Of dreams and the ruins of stars, having the same fate,
Obeying the same rules, in their descent, are alike?
Where was it written that such a night would spread,

Darkly inscribing itself everywhere, or for that matter, where
Was it written that I would be born into myself again and again,
As I am even now, as everything is at this moment,
And feel the fall of flesh into time, and feel it turn,
Soundlessly, slowly, as if righting itself, into line?

ONE WINTER NIGHT

I showed up at a party of Hollywood stars
Who milled about, quoted their memoirs, and drank.
The prettiest one stepped out of her dress, fell
To her knees and said that only her husband had glimpsed
The shadowy flower of her pudendum, and he was a prince.
A slip of sunlight rode the swell of her breasts
Into the blinding links of her necklace, and crashed.
Out on the lawn, the Platters were singing "Twilight Time."
"Heavenly shades of night are falling . . ." This was a dream.

Later, I went to the window and gazed at a bull, huge and pink,
In a field of snow. Moonlight poured down his back, and the damp
Of his breath spread until he was wreathed in a silver steam.
When he lifted his head, he loosed a bellow that broke and rolled
Like thunder in the rooms below. This, too, was a dream.

DANSE D'HIVER

We've seen them all: the torments of distance,
The sleepy renewals, the fair turning foul,
The line of buildings high in the falling snow,
Down an alley in the center of town
The old gang huddled around a fire,
The new gang warming their hands on each other.

Oh for the moon's displays of pallor.
Oh for the life of the people next door.
The alley points one way but what points the other?
If we should lose ourselves in this weather,
Will anyone know us when we arrive?
Will Mother and Father feed us or let us go?

THE EMPIRE OF CHANCE

Its terrain is dry and spreads out so you glimpse only bits
At a time; its cities have been known to shine,
But are usually hidden, appearing, suddenly
And by accident, around a bend.
I live near the mountains in a barren
Valley spread with boulders round and red.
I work a field that dims and disappears,
Then circles back to greet me. And after work,
I often sit in the emerald evening air,
My legs stretched out before me,
The collar of my coat turned up,
The wicker chair tilted back,
And wonder what they do up there
In the crystal hills, so cold, so filled
With the lack of what we have down here.
The sound of distant trains, their long
Monotonous whistles, floats down the frozen passes.
And in the dark, under the pressure of starlight,
I dream I'm somewhere else: I hear the sea heaving itself
Upon the shore and the sheer wind
Threading its way through patches of stunted pine
And layers of misted air. And while I strain
To keep that prospect near,
The small night garden behind the house
Sheds its scented moonlit flesh.
                              When daybreak comes,
The grassless plain beyond my field
Turns grayish pink, the moon's old face
Is pitted and blind, and a few clouds drag
Their skirts of rain.
And in the unshakable flush

Of sunlight curving down
To take me in, everything spins
Away, beyond my reach, as if my being here
Were some mistake. So the day begins.
The great lake to the west sends up a wall of haze,
The mountains to the south and east a frieze
Of snowy peaks, and the airy reaches
To the north a bank of cold.
Despite its ancient bounds, the empire has no shape.
I work my plot under the screech of gulls
And the sky's deep stare. I work myself
Until I cannot bear my work.
It is the hard truth of what I do.
My shadow shudders in the morning air.

TRANSLATION

1

A few months ago my four-year-old son surprised me. He was hunched over, polishing my shoes, when he looked up and said, "My translations of Palazzeschi are going poorly."

I quickly withdrew my foot. "Your translations? I didn't know you could translate."

"You haven't been paying much attention to me lately," he said. "I've been having a terrible time deciding what I want my translations to sound like. The closer I look at them, the less certain I am of how they are to be read or understood. And since I am just a beginning poet, the more like my poems they are, the less likely they are to be any good. I work and work, endlessly changing this or that, hoping by some miracle to arrive at just the right rendering of them in an English beyond my abilities to imagine. Oh, Dad, it's been hard."

The vision of my son struggling over Palazzeschi brought tears to my eyes. "Son," I said, "you should find a young poet to translate, someone your own age, whose poems are no good. Then, if your translations are bad, it won't matter."

2

My son's nursery school teacher came over to see me. "I don't know German," she said, as she unbuttoned her blouse and unsnapped her bra, letting them fall to the floor. "But I feel that I must translate Rilke. None of the translations I've read seems very good. If I pooled them, I'm sure I could come up with something better." She dropped her skirt. "I've heard that Rilke is the German Gerard Manley Hopkins, so I'll keep 'The Wreck of the Deutschland' on my desk as I work. Some of it is bound to rub off. I'm not sure which poems I'll do, but I favor the 'Duino Elegies,' since they are more like my own poems. Of course, I'll be taking German lessons while I work." She took off her panties. "Well, what do you think?" she asked as she stood naked before me.

"You are one of those," I said, "who believes translation is a reading not of the original, but of every available translated text. Why waste money on German lessons, if the actual source of your translation will be already finished translations?" Then, reaching out to shoo a fly from her hair, I said, "Your approach is the editorial one—you edit somebody else's translation until it sounds like yours, bypassing the most important stage in the conversion of one poem to another, which is the initial one of finding rough equivalents, the one which will contain the originality of your reading. Even if you work with someone who knows German, you will be no more than that person's editor, for he will have taken the initial step, and no matter how wisely he rationalizes his choice, it will have been made intuitively or automatically."

"I see your point," she said. "Maybe I should take a stab at Baudelaire."

3

"What's up?" I said to the nursery teacher's husband.

"I have decided not to translate in order to save my marriage," he said. "I'd thought of doing Jorge de Lima's poems, but didn't know how." He dabbed his sweaty upper lip with a crumpled hankie. "I thought perhaps that a translation should sound like a translation, reminding the reader that what he was reading had a prior life in another language and was not conceived in English. But I couldn't bring myself to write in a way that would remind somebody that what he was reading was better before I got hold of it. Dignifying the poem at the cost of the translation seems just as perverse as erasing the original with a translation. Not only that," he said, this time dabbing my upper lip with his hankie, and brushing my cheek with the back of his hand, "but if the dominant poetic idiom of a period determines how a poem is to be translated (and it usually does), it will also determine which poems should be translated. That is, in a period of muttering plain-style lyrics, baroque formulations of a performative sort will not be looked on favorably. So what should the translator do? Should he adopt an antique style? Or would that parody the vitality, ingenuity, and period naturalness of the original? Though de Lima is a twentieth-century poet, his brand of modernism is passé, quite out of keeping with the poetry being written today. So far as I can see, there's nothing to be done with his poems." And with that he disappeared down the street.

4

To get away from all the talk of translation I went camping by myself in southern Utah, and was about to light the campfire when a bare-chested man crawled out from the tent next to mine, stood, and started to file his nails. "You don't know who I am," he said, "but I know who you are."

"Who are you?" I asked.

"I'm Bob," he said. "I spent the first twenty years of my life in Porto Velho, and feel that Manuel Bandeira is the great undiscovered twentieth-century poet, undiscovered, that is, by the English-speaking world. I want to translate him." Then he narrowed his eyes. "I teach Portuguese at Southern Utah State, where the need for Portuguese is great, since so few people there seem to know it exists. You're not going to like this, but I don't go in for contemporary American poetry and don't see why that should disqualify me from translating. I can always get one of the local poets to look over what I've done. For me, meaning is the important thing."

Stunned by his penciled-in eyebrows and tiny mustache, I said, a bit unfairly, "You language teachers are all alike. You possess a knowledge of the original language and, perhaps, some knowledge of English, but that's it. The chances are your translations will be word-for-word renderings without the character or feel of poetry. You are the first to declare the impossibility of translating, but you think nothing of minimizing its difficulty." And with that I packed my things, struck the tent, and drove back to Salt Lake City.

5

I was in the bathtub when Jorge Luis Borges stumbled in the door. "Borges, be careful," I yelled. "The floor is slippery and you are blind." Then, soaping my chest, I said, "Borges, have you ever considered what is implicit in a phrase like 'I translate Apollinaire into English' or 'I translate de la Mare into French,' that we take the highly idiosyncratic work of an individual and render it into a language that belongs to everyone and to no one, a system of meanings sufficiently general to permit not only misunderstandings but to throw into doubt the possibility of permitting anything else?"

"Yes," he said with an air of resignation.

"Then don't you think," I said, "that the translation of poetry is best left to poets who are in possession of an English they have each made their own, and that language teachers, who feel responsibility to a language not in its modifications but in its monolithic entirety make the worst translators? Wouldn't it be best to think of translation as a transaction between individual idioms, between, say, the Italian of D'Annunzio and the English of Auden? If we did, we could end irrelevant discussions of who has and who hasn't done a correct translation."

"Yes," he said, seeming to get excited.

"Say," I said. "If translation is a kind of reading, the assumption or transformation of one personal idiom into another, then shouldn't it be possible to translate work done in one's own language? Shouldn't it be possible to translate Wordsworth or Shelley into Strand?"

"You will discover," said Borges, "that Wordsworth refuses to be translated. It is you who must be translated, who must become, for however long, the author of *The Prelude*. That is what happened to Pierre Menard when he translated Cervantes. He did not want to compose another *Don Quixote*—which would be easy— but *the Don Quixote*. His admirable ambition was to produce pages which would coincide—word for word and line for line—with those of Miguel de Cervantes. The initial method he conceived was relatively simple: to know Spanish well, to re-embrace the Catholic faith, to fight against the Moors and Turks, to forget European history between 1602 and 1918, and to *be* Miguel de Cervantes. To compose *Don Quixote* at the beginning of the seventeenth century was a reasonable, necessary, and perhaps inevitable undertaking; at the beginning of the twentieth century it was almost impossible."

"Not almost impossible," I said, "but absolutely impossible, for in order to translate, one must cease to be." I closed my eyes for a second and realized that if I ceased to be, I would never know. "Borges . . ." I was about to tell him that the strength of a style must be measured by its resistance to translation. "Borges . . ." But when I opened my eyes, he, and the text into which he was drawn, had come to an end.

THE HISTORY OF POETRY

Our masters are gone and if they returned
Who among us would hear them, who would know
The bodily sound of heaven or the heavenly sound
Of the body, endless and vanishing, that tuned
Our days before the wheeling stars
Were stripped of power? The answer is
None of us here. And what does it mean if we see
The moon-glazed mountains and the town with its silent doors
And water towers, and feel like raising our voices
Just a little, or sometimes during late autumn
When the evening flowers a moment over the western range
And we imagine angels rushing down the air's cold steps
To wish us well, if we have lost our will,
And do nothing but doze, half-hearing the sighs
Of this or that breeze drift aimlessly over the failed farms
And wasted gardens? These days when we waken,
Everything shines with the same blue light
That filled our sleep moments before,
So we do nothing but count the trees, the clouds,
The few birds left; then we decide that we shouldn't
Be hard on ourselves, that the past was no better
Than now, for hasn't the enemy always existed,
And wasn't the church of the world already in ruins?

THE CONTINENTAL COLLEGE OF BEAUTY

When the Continental College of Beauty opened its doors
We looked down hallways covered with old masters
And into rooms where naked figures lounged on marble floors.
And we were moved, but not enough to stay. We hurried on
Until we reached a courtyard overgrown with weeds.
This moved us, too, but in a moment we were nodding off.
The sun was coming up, a violet haze was lifting from the sea,
Coastal hills were turning red, and several people on the beach
Went up in flames. This was the start of something new.
The flames died down. The sun continued on its way.
And lakes inland, in the first light, flashed their scales,
And mountains cast a blue, cold shade on valley floors,
And distant towns awoke . . . this is what we'd waited for.
How quickly the great unfinished world came into view
When the Continental College of Beauty opened its doors.

THE MIDNIGHT CLUB

The gifted have told us for years that they want to be loved
For what they are, that they, in whatever fullness is theirs,
Are perishable in twilight, just like us. So they work all night
In rooms that are cold and webbed with the moon's light;
Sometimes, during the day, they lean on their cars,
And stare into the blistering valley, glassy and golden,
But mainly they sit, hunched in the dark, feet on the floor,
Hands on the table, shirts with a bloodstain over the heart.

THE FAMOUS SCENE

The polished scarlets of sunset sink as failure
Darkens the famous scene: nature's portrait of us
On the shore while the flooding sun soils the palms
And wooden walks before the rows of tiny summer homes.
Oh, and the silent birds are hunched in the trees
Or waiting under the eaves, and over there a boat
Cuts through the swell, releasing its coils of steam.
What does it mean to have come here so late?
Shall we know before the night wind strays
Into town, leaving a sea-stale wake, and we close
Our eyes against desire's incoming tides?
Probably not. So let the unsayable have its way.
Let the moon rage and fade, as it will, and the heads
Of Queen Anne's lace bow down in the fields,
And the dark be praised. We shall be off,
Talking aloud to ourselves, repeating the words
That have always been used to describe our fate.

ITSELF NOW

They will say it is feeling or mood, or the world, or the sound
The world makes on summer nights while everyone sleeps—
Trees awash with wind, something like that, something
As imprecise. But don't be fooled. The world
Is only a mirror returning its image. They will say
It is about particulars, making a case for this or that,
But it tries only to be itself. The low hills, the freshets,
The long dresses, even the lyre and dulcimer mean nothing,
The music it makes is mainly its own. So far
From what it might be, it always turns into longing,
Spinning itself out for desire's sake, desire for its own end,
One word after another erasing the world and leaving instead
The invisible lines of its calling: Out there, out there.

READING IN PLACE

Imagine a poem that starts with a couple
Looking into a valley, seeing their house, the lawn
Out back with its wooden chairs, its shady patches of green,
Its wooden fence, and beyond the fence the rippled silver sheen
Of the local pond, its far side a tangle of sumac, crimson
In the fading light. Now imagine somebody reading the poem
And thinking, "I never guessed it would be like this,"
Then slipping it into the back of a book while the oblivious
Couple, feeling nothing is lost, not even the white
Streak of a flicker's tail that catches their eye, nor the slight
Toss of leaves in the wind, shift their gaze to the wooden dome
Of a nearby hill where the violet spread of dusk begins.
But the reader, out for a stroll in the autumn night, with all
The imprisoned sounds of nature dying around him, forgets
Not only the poem, but where he is, and thinks instead
Of a bleak Venetian mirror that hangs in a hall
By a curving stair, and how the stars in the sky's black glass
Sink down and the sea heaves them ashore like foam.
So much is adrift in the ever-opening rooms of elsewhere,
He cannot remember whose house it was, or when he was there.
Now imagine he sits years later under a lamp
And pulls a book from the shelf; the poem drops
To his lap. The couple are crossing a field
On their way home, still feeling that nothing is lost,
That they will continue to live harm-free, sealed
In the twilight's amber weather. But how will the reader know,
Especially now that he puts the poem, without looking,
Back in the book, the book where a poet stares at the sky
And says to a blank page, "Where, where in heaven am I?"

THE END

Not every man knows what he shall sing at the end,
Watching the pier as the ship sails away, or what it will seem like
When he's held by the sea's roar, motionless, there at the end,
Or what he shall hope for once it is clear that he'll never go back.

When the time has passed to prune the rose or caress the cat,
When the sunset torching the lawn and the full moon icing it down
No longer appear, not every man knows what he'll discover instead.
When the weight of the past leans against nothing, and the sky

Is no more than remembered light, and the stories of cirrus
And cumulus come to a close, and all the birds are suspended in flight,
Not every man knows what is waiting for him, or what he shall sing
When the ship he is on slips into darkness, there at the end.

DARK HARBOR

PROEM

"This is my Main Street," he said as he started off
That morning, leaving the town to the others,
Entering the high woods tipped in pink

By the rising sun but still dark where he walked.
"This is the way," he continued as he watched
For the great space that he felt sure

Would open before him, a stark sea over which
The turbulent sky would drop the shadowy shapes
Of its song, and he would move his arms

And begin to mark, almost as a painter would,
The passages of greater and lesser worth, the silken
Tropes and calls to this or that, coarsely conceived,

Echoing and blasting all around. He would whip them
Into shape. Everything would have an edge. The burning
Will of weather, blowing overhead, would be his muse.

"This is the life," he said, as he reached the first
Of many outer edges to the sea he sought, and he buttoned
His coat, and turned up his collar, and began to breathe.

I

In the night without end, in the soaking dark,
I am wearing a white suit that shines
Among the black leaves falling, among

The insect-covered moons of the streetlamps.
I am walking among the emerald trees
In the night without end. I am crossing

The street and disappearing around the corner.
I shine as I go through the park on my way
To the station where the others are waiting.

Soon we shall travel through the soundless dark,
With fires guiding us over the bitter terrain
Of the night without end. I am wearing

A suit that outdoes the moon, that is pure sheen
As I come to the station where the others
Are whispering, saying that the moon

Is no more a hindrance than anything else,
That, if anyone suffers, wings can be had
For a song or by trading arms, that the rules

On earth still hold for those about to depart,
That it is best to be ready, for the ash
Of the body is worthless and goes only so far.

II

I am writing from a place you have never been,
Where the trains don't run, and planes
Don't land, a place to the west,

Where heavy hedges of snow surround each house,
Where the wind screams at the moon's blank face,
Where the people are plain, and fashions,

If they come, come late and are seen
As forms of oppression, sources of sorrow.
This is a place that sparkles a bit at 7 p.m.,

Then goes out, and slides into the funeral home
Of the stars, and everyone dreams of floating
Like angels in sweet-smelling habits,

Of being released from sundry services
Into the round of pleasures there for the asking—
Days like pages torn from a family album,

Endless reunions, the heavenly choir at the barbecue
Adjusting its tone to serve the occasion,
And everyone staring, stunned into magnitude.

III

Go in any direction and you will return to the main drag.
Something about the dull little shops, the useless items
That turn into necessities, a sense of direction,

Even the feel of becoming yourself on your return,
As you pass through the outskirts, the rows of houses
Aglow with an icy green from TVs, spreading

A sheen of familiarity, of deliverance, as you
Make your way back to the center where, because of the hour
The streets are deserted except for the slow passage of cars,

And here and there somebody standing for no reason,
Holding a letter in her hand or holding a leash
With no dog at the end, casting a shadow,

And you pass by unsure if this coming back is a failure
Or a sign of success, a sign that the time has come
To embrace your origins as you would yourself,

That staying away no longer makes sense, even if no one
Is shedding tears over the folly or wisdom of your decision;
The world has always gotten along without you,

Which is why you left home in the first place,
So what about those shops and the empty luminous cones
Of light that fall from the lamps, and the echo of your own steps?

From far away, life looked to be simpler back in the town
You started from . . . look, there in the kitchen are Mom and Dad,
He's reading the paper, she's killing a fly.

IV

There is a certain triviality in living here,
A lightness, a comic monotony that one tries
To undermine with shows of energy, a devotion

To the vagaries of desire, whereas over there
Is a seriousness, a stiff, inflexible gloom
That shrouds the disappearing soul, a weight

That shames our lightness. Just look
Across the river and you will discover
How unworthy you are as you describe what you see,

Which is bound by what is available.
On the other side, no one is looking this way.
They are committed to obstacles,

To the textures and levels of darkness,
To the tedious enactment of duration.
And they labor not for bread or love

But to perpetuate the balance between the past
And the future. They are the future as it
Extends itself, just as we are the past

Coming to terms with itself. Which is why
The napkins are pressed, and why the cookies have come
On time, and why the glass of milk, looking so chic

In its whiteness, begs us to sip. None of this happens
Over there, Relief from anything is seen
As timid, a sign of shallowness or worse.

V

The soldiers are gone, and now the women are leaving.
The dogs howl at the moon, and the moon flees
Through the clouds. I wonder if I shall ever catch up.

I think of the shining cheeks, the serious palettes
Of my friends, and I am sure I am not of their company.
There was a time when I was touched by the pallor of truth,

When the fatal steps I took seemed more like the drift
Of summer crossed at times by the scented music of rain,
But that was before I was waved to the side

By the officer on duty, and told that henceforth
I would have to invent my pleasure, carve it out of the air,
Subtract it from my future. And I could have no illusions;

A mysterious crape would cover my work. The roll of a drum
Would govern the fall of my feet in the long corridors.
"And listen," the officer said, "on any morning look down

Into the valley. Watch the shadows, the clouds dispersing
Then look through the ice into nature's frozen museum,
See how perfectly everything fits in its space."

VI

Where would it end and how would it matter
If the world, illumined by the dawning moon,
Were to break in on everyone's sleep,

And desire that is everywhere in dreams were released
And reached not for the whole earth which everyone
Thinks is its likely object, but instead grew

Into an enlarged desire, a desire that wished for even more,
For an unthinkable conclusion, an impossible satisfaction,
Itself increasing, enclosing within its appetite

The elaboration and extension of its despair,
The dark underside of growth that says to the pleasure
Of wishing there will be no satisfaction adequate,

That even on these silver lawns and sidewalks,
For which the midnight air of late October seems
The only possible accompaniment, no sign

Of satisfaction is possible. There is only
Larger and larger dissatisfaction. Only teeth
Tearing and gnawing. Everything always larger and more

Elusive, with the weight of the future saying
That I am only what you are, but more so.
And you, without allowing yourself time

For exhaustion, pursue this promise because
It is yours, the loss that is continuous
Will be all yours and will only increase.

VII

O you can make fun of the splendors of moonlight,
But what would the human heart be if it wanted
Only the dark, wanted nothing on earth

But the sea's ink or the rock's black shade?
On a summer night to launch yourself into the silver
Emptiness of air and look over the pale fields

At rest under the sullen stare of the moon,
And to linger in the depths of your vision and wonder
How in this whiteness what you love is past

Grief, and how in the long valley of your looking
Hope grows, and there, under the distant,
Barely perceptible fire of all the stars,

To feel yourself wake into change, as if your change
Were immense and figured into the heavens' longing.
And yet all you want is to rise out of the shade

Of yourself into the cooling blaze of a summer night
When the moon shines and the earth itself
Is covered and silent in the stoniness of its sleep.

VIII

If dawn breaks the heart, and the moon is a horror,
And the sun is nothing but the source of torpor,
Then of course I would have been silent all these years

And would not have chosen to go out tonight
In my new dark blue double-breasted suit
And to sit in a restaurant with a bowl

Of soup before me to celebrate how good life
Has been and how it has culminated in this instant.
The harmonies of wholesomeness have reached their apogee,

And I am aquiver with satisfaction, and you look
Good, too. I love your gold teeth and your dyed hair—
A little green, a little yellow—and your weight,

Which is finally up where we never thought
It would be. O my partner, my beautiful death,
My black paradise, my fusty intoxicant,

My symbolist muse, give me your breast
Or your hand or your tongue that sleeps all day
Behind its wall of reddish gums.

Lay yourself down on the restaurant floor
And recite all that's been kept from my happiness.
Tell me I have not lived in vain, that the stars

Will not die, that things will stay as they are,
That what I have seen will last, that I was not born
Into change, that what I have said has not been said for me.

IX

Where is the experience that meant so much,
That carried such weight? Where is it now
If not lodged in memory, in the air of memory,

In the place that is not a place, but where
The mortal beauty of the world is stored.
Oh yes, we are busy under the moon's gaze,

Its mouth giving back a silent O of surprise
Each time we try to explain how it was,
How fleeting, breakable, expensive it was.

We are always about to take off into a future
Unencumbered, as if we could leave ourselves behind,
But of course we never do. Who can face the future,

Especially now, as a nobody with no past
To fall back on, nothing to prove one is
Like everyone else, with baby pictures

And pictures of Mom and Dad in their old-fashioned
Swimsuits on a beach somewhere in the Maritimes.
We are at work on the past to make the future

More bearable. Ah, the potential past, how it swells,
How it crowds the days before us with feelings
And postures we had dismissed until now.

X

It is a dreadful cry that rises up,
Hoping to be heard, that comes to you
As you wake, so your day will be spent

In the futile correction of a distant longing.
All those voices calling from the depths of elsewhere,
From the abyss of an August night, from the misery

Of a northern winter, from a ship going down in the Baltic,
From heartache, from wherever you wish, calling to be saved.
And you have no choice but to follow their prompting,

Saving something of that sound, urging the harsh syllables
Of disaster into music. You stare out the window,
Watching the buildup of clouds, and the wind whipping

The branches of a willow, sending a rain of leaves
To the ground. How do you turn pain
Into its own memorial, how do you write it down,

Turning it into itself as witnessed
Through pleasure, so it can be known, even loved,
As it lives in what it could not be.

XI

A long time has passed and yet it seems
Like yesterday, in the midmost moment of summer,
When we felt the disappearance of sorrow,

And saw beyond the rough stone walls
The flesh of clouds, heavy with the scent
Of the southern desert, rise in a prodigal

Overflowing of mildness. It seems like yesterday
When we stood by the iron gate in the center
Of town while the pollen-filled breath

Of the wind drew the shadow of the clouds
Around us so that we could feel the force
Of our freedom while still the captives of dark.

And later when the rain fell and flooded the streets
And we heard the dripping on the porch and the wind
Rustling the leaves like paper, how to explain

Our happiness then, the particular way our voices
Erased all signs of the sorrow that had been,
Its violence, its terrible omens of the end?

XII

So it came of its own like the sun that covers
The damp grass with its luster and drives the cold
Into the dark corners of the house; out of silence

It came, and, as we were not exactly wild
With anticipation, it waited awhile at the verge
Of recognition, growing in importance

And urgency but still without a message
To deliver, until the wind blew just so
And formed a formidable cat's-paw

On the water, at which point for some reason,
We knew it had come at last—the sense that we were
To make of such an appearance, its sudden arrival,

How it crowded out everything else. And now
The panorama of the lake was charged
With the arrival of a cloud whose purpose

We would have to decipher and apply
To our own ends, so we could say that it came
For further clarification, some heavy editing,

As it pitched itself forward, casting a shade,
A vague sense, over the lake and us,
Which would end in either dismissal or doubt.

XIII

The mist clears. The morning mountains
Range themselves beyond the placid town.
The light-footed deer come down to the graveyard,

And the magpies cry. All is well.
It is the moment to resist the onset
Of another average day, to beat the daylight

For exotic instances of this or that.
We must let out the pigs, pink and snorting,
To wander the neighborhood, we must

Let out the cows as well, and let them
Lounge on the lawns of the major houses,
There's lots to be done. For instance,

Make imprecision the core of the school
Curriculum so that years from now we will appear
Unchanged, make sadness another required course,

So that it can be known without
Personal involvement. There is little time left.
None for a drink at the local bistro,

None for a pointless stroll, none for a change
Of clothes. We must get down to work: mail the pajamas
To Esther in Holland, paint the sidewalk,

Move the dying piano out to the beach.
If only it were possible to spruce up the air
Without buying a spruce, the day might begin

To take on a light of its own, green and piercing.

XIV

The ship has been held in the harbor.
The promise of departure has begun to dim.
The radiance of the sea, the shining abundance

Of its blue are nevertheless undiminished.
The will of the passengers struggles to release
The creaking ship. All they want

Is one last voyage beyond the papery palms
And the shoals of melancholy, beyond the glass
And alabaster mansions strung along

The shore, beyond the siren sounds
And the grinding gears of big trucks climbing the hills,
Out into the moonlit bareness of waves,

Where watery scrawls tempt the voyager to reach down
And hold the dissolving messages in his palm.
Again and again the writing surfaces,

Shines a moment in the light, then sinks unread.
Why should the passengers want so badly
To glimpse what they shall never have?

Why are so many of them crowded at the rail,
With the ship still dozing in the harbor?
And to whom are they waving? It has been

Years since the stores in town were open,
Years since the flag was raised in the little park,
Since the cloud behind the nearby mountain moved.

XV

What light is this that says the air is golden,
That even the green trees can be saved
For a moment and look bejeweled,

That my hand, as I lift it over the shade
Of my body, becomes a flame pointing the way
To a world from which no one returns, yet toward

Which everyone travels? The sheen of the possible
Is adjusting itself to a change of venue: the look
Of farewell, the sun dipping under the clouds,

Faltering at the serrated edge of the mountains,
Then going quickly. And the new place, the night,
Spacious, empty, a tomb of lights, turning away,

And going under, becoming what no one remembers.

XVI

It is true, as someone has said, that in
A world without heaven all is farewell.
Whether you wave your hand or not,

It is farewell, and if no tears come to your eyes
It is still farewell, and if you pretend not to notice,
Hating what passes, it is still farewell.

Farewell no matter what. And the palms as they lean
Over the green, bright lagoon, and the pelicans
Diving, and the glistening bodies of bathers resting,

Are stages in an ultimate stillness, and the movement
Of sand, and of wind, and the secret moves of the body
Are part of the same, a simplicity that turns being

Into an occasion for mourning, or into an occasion
Worth celebrating, for what else does one do,
Feeling the weight of the pelicans' wings,

The density of the palms' shadows, the cells that darken
The backs of bathers? These are beyond the distortions
Of chance, beyond the evasions of music. The end

Is enacted again and again. And we feel it
In the temptations of sleep, in the moon's ripening,
In the wine as it waits in the glass.

XVII

I have just said goodbye to a friend
And am staring at fields of cornstalks.
Their stubble is being burned, and the smoke

Forms a gauze over the sun's blank face.
Off to the side there is a line of poplars.
And beyond, someone is driving a tractor.

Does he live in that little white house?
Someone is playing a tape of birds singing.
Someone has fallen asleep on a boxcar of turnips.

I think of the seasonal possibilities.
O pretty densities of white on white!
O snowflake lost in the vestibules of April air!

Beyond the sadness—the empty restaurants,
The empty streets, the small lamps shining
Down on the town—I see only the stretches

Of ice and snow, the straight pines, the frigid moon.

XVIII

"I would like to step out of my heart's door and be
Under the great sky." I would like to step out
And be on the other side, and be part of all

That surrounds me. I would like to be
In that solitude of soundless things, in the random
Company of the wind, to be weightless, nameless.

But not for long, for I would be downcast without
The things I keep inside my heart; and in no time
I would be back. Ah! the old heart

In which I sleep, in which my sleep increases, in which
My grief is ponderous, in which the leaves are falling,
In which the streets are long, in which the night

Is dark, in which the sky is great, the old heart
That murmurs to me of what cannot go on,
Of the dancing, of the inmost dancing.

XIX

I go out and sit on my roof, hoping
That a creature from another planet will see me
And say, "There's life on earth, definitely life;

"See that earthling on top of his home,
His manifold possessions under him,
Let's name him after our planet." Whoa!

XX

Is it you standing among the olive trees
Beyond the courtyard? You in the sunlight
Waving me closer with one hand while the other

Shields your eyes from the brightness that turns
All that is not you dead white? Is it you
Around whom the leaves scatter like foam?

You in the murmuring night that is scented
With mint and lit by the distant wilderness
Of stars? Is it you? Is it really you

Rising from the script of waves, the length
Of your body casting a sudden shadow over my hand
So that I feel how cold it is as it moves

Over the page? You leaning down and putting
Your mouth against mine so I should know
That a kiss is only the beginning

Of what until now we could only imagine?
Is it you or the long compassionate wind
That whispers in my ear: alas, alas?

XXI

Low shadows skim the earth, a few clouds bleed,
A couple of grazing cows carry the next world
On their backs, their hides the mysterious maps

Of the principal countries. Too bad the future
Is covered with flies, and sits in a pasture.
Here comes old age, dragging a tale of soft

Inconvenience, of golfing in Florida,
Of gumming bad food. These cows never stop chewing.
O love, how did we get here, so far from the coast

Of our friends, our nervous talkative friends
Who are now reading in bed or watching TV
Because it is later there, and they must

Keep their minds off missing us, off whatever
Would happen were we to come back from our exile?
And the earth is almost dark, the crickets

Are clicking, the laundry is in the dryer,
The heat of the night is giving us new things
To wish for. Who cares if we were young once—

The young don't care, the old don't care,
So long as they are not left behind.

XXII

It happened years ago and in somebody else's
Dining room. Madame X begged to be relieved
Of a sexual pain that had my name

Written all over it. Those were the days
When so many things of a sexual nature seemed to happen,
And my name—I believed—was written on all of them.

Madame X took my hand under the table, placed it
On her thigh, then moved it up. You would never know
What a woman with such blue eyes and blond hair

Was not wearing. Did I suffer,
Knowing that I was wanted for the wrong reasons?
Of course, and it has taken me years to recover.

We don't give parties like that anymore.
These days we sit around and sigh.
We like the sound of it, and it seems to combine

Weariness and judgment, even to suggest
No eggs for the moment, no sausages either,
Just come, take me away, and put me to bed.

XXIII

And suddenly we heard the explosion.
A man who'd been cramped and bloated for weeks
Blew wide open. His wife, whose back was to him,

Didn't turn right away to give everything—
The cheese and soggy bread—a chance to settle.
She was a beauty, and considered a cunning cook,

But there were things she did not share with the rest of us.
So the fact that her back was turned was important.
We seemed to sense that she and her husband

Hadn't been seeing eye to eye. But that was as far as we got
Even though we questioned her culinary skills and what
Had driven her to blow up her husband, and we wondered—

Each of the men in the room—if she considered
Blowing us up. It happened that she left town
Before we could ask. No charges were pressed

So she sold the house and moved
To a large southern city where no one would know
The dangers of being invited to her house for dinner.

XXIV

Now think of the weather and how it is rarely the same
For any two people, how when it is small, precision is needed
To say when it is really an aura or odor or even an air

Of certainty, or how, as the hours go by, it could be thought of
As large because of the number of people it touches.
Its strength is something else: tornadoes are small

But strong and cloudless summer days seem infinite
But tend to be weak since we don't mind being out in them.
Excuse me, is this the story of another exciting day,

The sort of thing that accompanies preparations for dinner?
Then what say we talk about the inaudible—the shape it assumes,
And what social implications it holds,

Or the somber flourishes of autumn—the bright
Or blighted leaves falling, the clicking of cold branches,
The new color of the sky, its random blue.

XXV

Is what exists a souvenir of the time
Of the great nought and deep night without stars.
The time before the universe began?

When we look at each other and see nothing
Is that not a confirmation that we are less
Than meets the eye and embody some of

The night of our origins, and isn't everything
A little less than meets the eye, reminding us
That our ignorance is verified by the nothing

Which it honors? And isn't it true that
A loss of memory is the most powerful force
In the formation of culture, that the past

Is always simplified to make room for
The present? And aren't we more interested
In what may happen or will happen

Than in what has already happened, and so look ahead
Into the dark and imagine a fullness in which
We are the stars, matching the emptiness

Of the beginning, giving birth to ourselves
Again and again, rising out of the ruins or ashes
Of the past? Our images blaze a path

That our poor bodies must follow. And the wind
That pursues is the perfumed wind of spring
That promises much, but settles for summer.

XXVI

I have come from my cabin, from my place high
In the Rockies, have trod down narrow gravel trails,
Slogged through bogs and mudflats, have come

Into the broad valley and, without food
And drink, crossed it, and all the while
Murmured your name to myself, and as I did

I was filled with a shuddering, something
Like ecstasy, and was on the verge of losing
My way, but never did; I just kept coming;

Nothing could hold me back, not the sudden
Soaking downpours, not the stretches of clogging heat,
Nothing. I staggered forward, unshaven, limping,

My clothes ragged, I came in my vileness, believing
That you, understanding my passion, would forgive me,
And after the reading, O my master, that you would

Open the copy of your book, which I brought with me,
Taped to my back so that it wouldn't get
Dirty or stolen, and sign it and say a kind word

Or offer best wishes to me, one of the many
Worshippers of your work and himself a practitioner,
So that on the worst days it will be possible

For me to open it and feel wanted, and to know,
In my lingering over your signature, Master, the power
Of your wisdom as you have passed it on to me.

XXVII

Of this one I love how the beautiful echoed
Within the languorous length of his sentences,
Forming a pleasing pointless commotion;

Of another the figures pushing each other
Out of the way, the elaborate overcharged
Thought threatening always to fly apart;

Of another the high deliberate tone,
The diction tending toward falseness
But always falling perfectly short;

Of another the rush and vigor of observation,
The speed of disclosure, the aroused intelligence
Exerting itself, lifting the poem into prophecy;

Of this one the humor, the struggle to locate high art
Anywhere but expected, and to gild the mundane
With the force of the demonic or the angelic;

Of yet another the precision, the pursuit of rightness,
Balance, some ineffable decorum, the measured, circuitous
Stalking of the subject, turning surprise to revelation;

And that leaves this one on the side of his mountain,
Hunched over the page, thanking his loves for coming
And keeping him company all this time.

XXVIII

There is a luminousness, a convergence of enchantments,
And the world is altered for the better as trees,
Rivers, mountains, animals, all find their true place,

But only while Orpheus sings. When the song is over
The world resumes its old flaws, and things are again
Mismatched and misplaced and the cruelty of men

Is tempered only by laws. Orpheus can change the world
For a while, but he cannot save it, which is his despair.
It is a brilliant limitation he enacts and

He knows it, which is why the current of his song
Is always mournful, always sad. It is even worse
For the rest of us. As someone has said, ". . . we barely begin

And paralysis takes over, forcing us out for a breath
Of fresh air." As if that wasn't bad enough, he says,
"But though reams of work do get done, not much listens.

I have the feeling my voice is just for me . . ." There is
A current of resignation that charges even our most
Determined productions. Still, we feel better for trying,

And there is always a glass of wine to restore us
To our former majesty, to the well of our wishes
In which we are mirrored, but darkly as though

A shadowed glass held within its frozen calm an image
Of abundance, a bloom of humanness, a hymn in which
The shapes and sounds of paradise are buried.

XXIX

The folded memory of our great and singular elevations,
The tragic slapping of vowels to produce tears,
The heavy golden grieving in our dreams,

Shaping the soul's solemn sounds on the edge of speech
That carry the fullness of intention and the emptiness
Of achievement are not quite the savage

Knowledge of ourselves that refuses to correct itself
But lumbers instead into formless affirmation,
Saying selfhood is hating Dad or wanting Mom,

Is being kissed by a reader somewhere, is about me
And all my minutes circulating around me like flies—
Me at my foulest, the song of me, me in the haunted

Woods of my own condition, a solitaire but never alone.
These are bad times. Idiots have stolen the moonlight.
They cast their shadowy pomp wherever they wish.

XXX

There is a road through the canyon,
A river beside the road, a forest.
If there is more, I haven't seen it yet.

Still, it is possible to say this has been
An amazing century for fashion if for nothing else;
The way brave models held back their tears

When thinking of the millions of Jews and Serbs
That Hitler killed, and how the photographer
Steadied his hand when he considered

The Muzhiks that Stalin took care of.
The way skirts went up and down; how breasts
Were in, then out; and the long and the short of hair.

But the road that winds through the canyon
Is covered with snow, and the river flows
Under the ice. Cross-country skiers are moving

Like secrets between the trees of the glassed-in forest.
The day has made a fabulous cage of cold around
My face. Whenever I take a breath I hear cracking.

XXXI

Here we are in Labrador. I've always
Wanted to be here, especially with you,
In this cabin, with a fire blazing. You are

Wearing a Calvin Klein suit and I am in
My father's velvet smoking jacket. That's all.
Why? Because I am happy. And I am ready

For the first sign from you that we should
Get into bed. These moments of giddy anticipation
Are the happiest of my life. I wonder if we

Are not part of someone's prediction of what
The world could be at its very best, if we,
In this frigid landscape free of shopping

Opportunities, are where the world is headed.
Or maybe we are part of the record of what
Has already happened, and are a sign of the depths

To which the world sank? Your costly suit,
My shabby jacket, this cabin without indoor
Plumbing or decent stove or stereo or TV

May be no more than a joke in the final
Tally of accomplishments to be claimed
At some late date. Still, here we are

And they can't take that away from us,
And if they laugh, so what, we're here,
Happy in Labrador, dancing into the wee hours.

XXXII

Out here, dwarfed by mountains and a sky of fires
And round rocks, in the academy of revelations
Which gets smaller every year, we have come

To see ourselves as less and do not like
Shows of abundance, descriptions we cannot believe,
When a simple still life—roses in an azure bowl—does fine.

The idea of our being large is inconceivable,
Even after lunch with Harry at Lutèce, even after
Finishing *The Death of Virgil*. The image of a god,

A platonic person, who does not breathe or bleed,
But brings whole rooms, whole continents to light,
Like the sun, is not for us. We have a growing appetite

For littleness, a piece of ourselves, a bit of the world,
An understanding that remains unfinished, unentire,
Largely imperfect so long as it lasts.

XXXIII

I was visiting the shabby villa of a friend,
Full of rooms curtained against the sun,
With marble floors uncarpeted and cold.

He had invited a few Russian women
For dinner. I remember liking the custard,
Which none of the other guests touched.

I felt alone. The women began to blow
Out the candles. I wondered if they, too, had been
To the Delicatessen of Love. No, they had been

To Italy, they said. When I returned to my room,
I put on my overcoat and got into bed.
Soon I heard a rustling outside my door.

"It's me, Olga, may I come in?" When she came in,
I got out of bed, took off my clothes, and stood
in front of the mirror. She joined me. "Finally,

We are safe from one another," she said. "Yes,"
I admitted somewhat sadly, "in the mirror the body
Becomes simultaneously visible and untouchable."

And so, in the gloomy villa we spent the night
Staring at our naked bodies, cold, shining,
While a fair fire roared in the hearth.

XXXIV

It's a pity that nature no longer means
The woods, nor the wilds, nor even our own
Worst behavior, nor the behavior of

Certain creatures. It's a pity we cannot
Believe that man and nature are essentially
Adapted to each other, that "the mind of man"

Mirrors "the fairest and most interesting
Qualities of nature." Now that nature includes
Oblivion, in which we dare not see ourselves,

We stand under the hollow moon and hear
No praising harp strings or mournful talk
To move us closer to the unreachables—

The silences and distances in which we walk
And feel ourselves available to all
That bends us toward each other.

The wind is hollow. The world is strange,
Part of an order, larger than and oblivious
To the life that gathers upon it.

XXXV

The sickness of angels is nothing new.
I have seen them crawling like bees,
Flightless, chewing their tongues, not singing,

Down by the bus terminal, hanging out,
Showing their legs, hiding their wings,
Carrying on for their brief term on earth,

No longer smiling; asleep in the shade of each other
They drift into the arms of strangers who step
Into their light, which is the mascara of Eden,

Offering more than invisible love,
Intangible comforts, offering the taste,
The pure erotic glory of death without echoes,

The feel of kisses blown out of heaven,
Melting the moment they land.

XXXVI

I cannot decide whether or not to stroll
Through the somber garden where the grass in the shade
Is silver and frozen and where the general green

Of the rest of the garden is dark except
For a luminous patch made by the light of a window.
I cannot decide, and because it is autumn

When the sadness of gardens is greatest, I believe
That someone is already there and waiting
For the pale appearance of another. She sits

On one of the benches, breathing the sweet
Rotten odors of leaves trapped under the trees, and feels
The sudden cold, a seasonal chill, the distant breath

Of coming rain. So many silent battles are waged
By those who sit alone and wait, and by those who delay.
By the time I arrive the snow has whitened my hair,

And placed on my shoulders two glittering, tiny
Epaulettes. I could be a major in Napoleon's army,
Which might be the reason she asks me:

Why would someone invade a poor country
Like this, a garden near the end of its life
With a woman inside it, unless he was lonely

And would do what he must to stave off the long
Campaigns of unhappiness that level everything,
Making rebuilding impossible, especially in winter?

XXXVII

On Sunday she sits in a silver chair in an echoing hall,
Wearing the cold clothes of a widow, as if she were one,
Hearing the cries of the wind among the twisted trees.

If there were someone there, she would speak
Of what it is like to wait without hope, to watch
The daylight inch across the floor,

Or maybe she would say that death is easier if everywhere
One looks is hell, and there is nowhere else to go.
Orpheus came to visit her, came several times.

Each time he left he wished her well, but he was a fool,
Preferring the moonlit chords of his melancholy,
The inward drift of notes to anything of hers. And yet,

What does it matter now? He's gone for good. The floating
Darkness of the cries seem more and more the prompting
Of a distant will, a fatal music rising everywhere.

XXXVIII

And so he appears at the back of the hall.
The rest is up to me. To say, for example,
Why he has come and where he has come from,

And why for this occasion he has chosen to wear
A hat when nobody these days wears a hat,
And why he wears it pulled down so the brim

Just clears his eyes. He never smiles,
He never shifts his weight. He merely stands
And stares as if in the severity

Of his motionlessness he were a stand-in
For somebody or something, an idea
Of withdrawal or silence, for instance,

Or for the perfection of watchfulness, how
It entraps by casting an invisible net
Around the watched, paralyzing him,

Turning him into a watcher as well,
A watcher who sees and must say what he sees,
Must carve a figure out of blankness,

Invent it in other words so that it has meaning,
Which is the burden of invention, its
Awkward weight, which must fit the man's

Appearance, the way he raises a hand
And extends it at arm's length, holding within it
A small gun, which he points at the one who assumed

The responsibility of watching, and now he squeezes
The trigger and the gun goes off and something falls,
A fragment, a piece of a larger intention, that is all.

XXXIX

When after a long silence one picks up the pen
And leans over the paper and says to himself:
Today I shall consider Marsyas

Whose body was flayed to excess,
Who made no crime that would square
With what he was made to suffer.

Today I shall consider the shredded remains of Marsyas—
What do they mean as they gather the sunlight
That falls in pieces through the trees,

As in Titian's late painting? Poor Marsyas,
A body, a body of work as it turns and falls
Into suffering, becoming the flesh of light,

Which is fed to onlookers centuries later.
Can this be the cost of encompassing pain?
After a long silence, would I, whose body

Is whole, sheltered, kept in the dark by a mind
That prefers it that way, know what I'd done
And what its worth was? Or is a body scraped

From the bone of experience, the chart of suffering
To be read in such ways that all flesh might be redeemed,
At least for the moment, the moment it passes into song.

XL

How can I sing when I haven't the heart, or the hope
That something of paradise persists in my song,
That a touch of those long afternoons of summer

Flowing with golden greens under the sky's unbroken blue
Will find a home in yet another imagined place?
Will someone be there to play the viola, someone for whom

The sad tunes still matter? And after I go, as I must,
And come back through the hourglass, will I have proved
That I live against time, that the silk of the songs

I sang is not lost? Or will I have proved that whatever I love
Is unbearable, that the views of Lethe will never
Improve, that whatever I sing is a blank?

XLI

Sometimes after dinner when I wander out,
And stare into the night sky and realize I have no idea
Of what I see, that the distance of the stars

Is meaningless and their number far beyond
What I can reckon, I wonder if the physicist
Sees the same sky I do, a lavish ordering of lights,

Disposed to match our scale, and our power to imagine
In simple terms a space like the space we suffer
Here on earth in this room with you sitting

In that chair, reading a book of which I understand
Nothing, thinking thoughts I could not guess at,
As moments approach whose cargo is a mystery.

Ah, who knows! We are already traveling faster than our
Apparent stillness can stand, and if it keeps up
You will be light-years away by the time I speak.

XLII

Our friends who lumbered from room to room
Now move like songs or meditations winding down,
Or lie about, waiting for the next good thing—

Some news of what is going on above,
A visitor to tell them who's writing well,
Who's falling in or out of love.

Not that it matters anymore. Just look around.
There's Marsyas, noted for his marvelous asides
On Athena's ancient oboe, asleep for centuries.

And Arion, whose gaudy music drove the Phrygians wild,
Hasn't spoken in a hundred years. The truth is
Soon the song deserts its maker,

The airy demon dies, and others come along.
A different kind of dark invades the autumn woods,
A different sound sends lovers packing into sleep.

The air is full of anguish. The measures of nothingness
Are few. The Beyond is merely beyond,
A melancholy place of failed and fallen stars.

XLIII

All afternoon I have thought how alike
Are "The Lament of the Pianos Heard in Rich Neighborhoods"
And "Piano Practice at the Academy of the Holy Angels,"

And how the girls that played are no longer here. Yet it was never
A vast music that mingled with the lusters of the room,
Nothing that would drown our desire for rest or silence.

It was just there like the source of delight—
Unblemished, unobserved—though things did not always turn out well.
As now the green leaves brood under an early snow,

And the houses are darkened by time. The sounds of summer
Have left. The purple woods, which color the distance,
Form a farewell for the monotonous autumn.

The snows have come, and the black shapes of the pianos
Are sleeping and cannot be roused, like the girls themselves
Who have gone, and the leaves, and all that was just here.

XLIV

I recall that I stood before the breaking waves,
Afraid not of the water so much as the noise,
That I covered my ears and ran to my mother

And waited to be taken away to the house in town
Where it was quiet, with no sound of the sea anywhere near.
Yet the sea itself, the sight of it, the way it spread

As far as we could see, was thrilling.
Only its roar was frightening. And now years later
It is the sound as well as its size that I love

And miss in my inland exile among the mountains
That do not change except for the light
That colors them or the snows that make them remote

Or the clouds that lift them, so they appear much higher
Than they are. They are acted upon and have none
Of the mystery of the sea that generates its own changes.

Encounters with each are bound to differ,
Yet if I had to choose I would look at the sea
And lose myself in its sounds which so frightened me once.

But in those days what did I know of the pleasures of loss,
Of the edge of the abyss coming close with its hisses
And storms, a great watery animal breaking itself on the rocks,

Sending up stars of salt, loud clouds of spume.

XLV

I am sure you would find it misty here,
With lots of stone cottages badly needing repair.
Groups of souls, wrapped in cloaks, sit in the fields

Or stroll the winding unpaved roads. They are polite,
And oblivious to their bodies, which the wind passes through,
Making a shushing sound. Not long ago,

I stopped to rest in a place where an especially
Thick mist swirled up from the river. Someone,
Who claimed to have known me years before,

Approached, saying there were many poets
Wandering around who wished to be alive again.
They were ready to say the words they had been unable to say—

Words whose absence had been the silence of love,
Of pain, and even of pleasure. Then he joined a small group,
Gathered beside a fire. I believe I recognized

Some of the faces, but as I approached they tucked
Their heads under their wings. I looked away to the hills
Above the river, where the golden lights of sunset

And sunrise are one and the same, and saw something flying
Back and forth, fluttering its wings. Then it stopped in midair.
It was an angel, one of the good ones, about to sing.

BLIZZARD OF ONE

I

UNTITLED

As for the poem the Adorable One slipped into your pocket,
Which began, "I think continually about us, the superhuman, how
We fly around saying, 'Hi, I'm So-and-So, and who are you?'"
It has been years since you bothered to read it. But now
In this lavender light under the shade of the pines the time
Seems right. The dust of a passion, the dark crumble of images
Down the page are all that remain. And she was beautiful,
And the poem, you thought at the time, was equally so.
The lavender turns to ash. The clouds disappear. Where
Is she now? And where is that boy who stood for hours
Outside her house, learning too late that something is always
About to happen just at the moment it serves no purpose at all?

THE BEACH HOTEL

Oh, look, the ship is sailing without us! And the wind
Is from the east, and the next ship leaves in a year.
Let's go back to the beach hotel where the rain never stops,
Where the garden, green and shadow-filled, says, in the rarest
Of whispers, "Beware of encroachment." We can stroll, can visit
The dead decked out in their ashen pajamas, and after a tour
Of the birches, can lie on the rumpled bed, watching
The ancient moonlight creep across the floor. The windowpanes
Will shake, and waves of darkness, cold, uncalled for, grim,
Will cover us. And into the close and mirrored catacombs of sleep
We'll fall, and there in the faded light discover the bones,
The dust, the bitter remains of someone who might have been
Had we not taken his place.

OLD MAN LEAVES PARTY

It was clear when I left the party
That though I was over eighty I still had
A beautiful body. The moon shone down as it will
On moments of deep introspection. The wind held its breath.
And look, somebody left a mirror leaning against a tree.
Making sure that I was alone, I took off my shirt.
The flowers of bear grass nodded their moon-washed heads.
I took off my pants and the magpies circled the redwoods.
Down in the valley the creaking river was flowing once more.
How strange that I should stand in the wilds alone with my body.
I know what you are thinking. I was like you once. But now
With so much before me, so many emerald trees, and
Weed-whitened fields, mountains and lakes, how could I not
Be only myself, this dream of flesh, from moment to moment?

I WILL LOVE THE TWENTY-FIRST CENTURY

Dinner was getting cold. The guests, hoping for quick,
Impersonal, random encounters of the usual sort, were sprawled
In the bedrooms. The potatoes were hard, the beans soft, the meat—
There was no meat. The winter sun had turned the elms and houses
    yellow;
Deer were moving down the road like refugees; and in the driveway,
    cats
Were warming themselves on the hood of a car. Then a man turned
And said to me: "Although I love the past, the dark of it,
The weight of it teaching us nothing, the loss of it, the all
Of it asking for nothing, I will love the twenty-first century more,
For in it I see someone in bathrobe and slippers, brown-eyed and poor,
Walking through snow without leaving so much as a footprint
    behind."
           "Oh," I said, putting my hat on, "oh."

THE NEXT TIME

I

Nobody sees it happening, but the architecture of our time
Is becoming the architecture of the next time. And the dazzle

Of light upon the waters is as nothing beside the changes
Wrought therein, just as our waywardness means

Nothing against the steady pull of things over the edge.
Nobody can stop the flow, but nobody can start it either.

Time slips by; our sorrows do not turn into poems,
And what is invisible stays that way. Desire has fled,

Leaving only a trace of perfume in its wake,
And so many people we loved have gone,

And no voice comes from outer space, from the folds
Of dust and carpets of wind to tell us that this

Is the way it was meant to happen, that if only we knew
How long the ruins would last we would never complain.

II

Perfection is out of the question for people like us,
So why plug away at the same old self when the landscape

Has opened its arms and given us marvelous shrines
To flock toward? The great motels to the west are waiting,

In somebody's yard a pristine dog is hoping that we'll drive by,
And on the rubber surface of a lake people bobbing up and down

Will wave. The highway comes right to the door, so let's
Take off before the world out there burns up. Life should be more

Than the body's weight working itself from room to room.
A turn through the forest will do us good, so will a spin

Among the farms. Just think of the chickens strutting,
The cows swinging their udders, and flicking their tails at flies.

And one can imagine prisms of summer light breaking against
The silent, haze-filled sleep of the farmer and his wife.

III

It could have been another story, the one that was meant
Instead of the one that happened. Living like this,

Hoping to revise what has been false or rendered unreadable
Is not what we wanted. Believing that the intended story

Would have been like a day in the west when everything
Is tirelessly present—the mountains casting their long shadow

Over the valley where the wind sings its circular tune
And trees respond with a dry clapping of leaves—was overly

Simple no doubt, and short-sighted. For soon the leaves,
Having gone black, would fall, and the annulling snow

Would pillow the walk, and we, with shovels in hand, would meet,
Bow, and scrape the sidewalk clean. What else would there be

This late in the day for us but desire to make amends
And start again, the sun's compassion as it disappears?

THE NIGHT, THE PORCH

To stare at nothing is to learn by heart
What all of us will be swept into, and baring oneself
To the wind is feeling the ungraspable somewhere close by.
Trees can sway or be still. Day or night can be what they wish.
What we desire, more than a season or weather, is the comfort
Of being strangers, at least to ourselves. This is the crux
Of the matter, which is why even now we seem to be waiting
For something whose appearance would be its vanishing—
The sound, say, of a few leaves falling, or just one leaf,
Or less. There is no end to what we can learn. The book out there
Tells us as much, and was never written with us in mind.

PRECIOUS LITTLE

for Bill and Sandy Bailey

If blindness is blind to itself
Then vision will come.
You open the door that was your shield,
And walk out into the coils of wind
And blurred tattoos of light that mar the ground.
The day feels cold on your skin.
"Out of my way," you say to whatever is waiting, "out of my way."
In a trice the purple thunder draws back, the tulip drops
Its petals, the path is clear.
You head west over the Great
Divide and down through canyons into an endless valley.
The air is pure, the houses are vacant.
Off in the distance the wind—all ice and feeling—
Invents a tree and a harp, and begins to play.
What could be better—long phrases of air stirring the leaves,
The leaves turning? But listen again. Is it really the wind,
Or is it the sound of somebody running
One step ahead of the dark?
And if it is, and nothing turns out
As you thought, then what is the difference
Between blindness lost and blindness regained?

THE GREAT POET RETURNS

When the light poured down through a hole in the clouds,
We knew the great poet was going to show. And he did.
A limousine with all-white tires and stained-glass windows
Dropped him off. And then, with a clear and soundless fluency,
He strode into the hall. There was a hush. His wings were big.
The cut of his suit, the width of his tie, were out of date.
When he spoke, the air seemed whitened by imagined cries.
The worm of desire bore into the heart of everyone there.
There were tears in their eyes. The great one was better than ever.
"No need to rush," he said at the close of the reading, "the end
Of the world is only the end of the world as you know it."
How like him, everyone thought. Then he was gone,
And the world was a blank. It was cold and the air was still.
Tell me, you people out there, what is poetry anyway?
        Can anyone die without even a little?

II

OUR MASTERPIECE IS THE PRIVATE LIFE

for Jules

I

Is there something down by the water keeping itself from us,
Some shy event, some secret of the light that falls upon the deep,
Some source of sorrow that does not wish to be discovered yet?

Why should we care? Doesn't desire cast its rainbows over the coarse
    porcelain
Of the world's skin and with its measures fill the air? Why look for
    more?

II

And now, while the advocates of awfulness and sorrow
Push their dripping barge up and down the beach, let's eat
Our brill, and sip this beautiful white Beaune.

True, the light is artificial, and we are not well dressed.
So what. We like it here. We like the bullocks in the field next door,
We like the sound of wind passing over grass. The way you speak,

In that low voice, our late-night disclosures . . . why live
For anything else? Our masterpiece is the private life.

III

Standing on the quay between the Roving Swan and the Star
    Immaculate,
Breathing the night air as the moment of pleasure taken
In pleasure vanishing seems to grow, its self-soiling

Beauty, which can only be what it was, sustaining itself
A little longer in its going, I think of our own smooth passage
Through the graded partitions, the crises that bleed

Into the ordinary, leaving us a little more tired each time,
A little more distant from the experiences, which, in the old days,
Held us captive for hours. The drive along the winding road

Back to the house, the sea pounding against the cliffs,
The glass of whiskey on the table, the open book, the questions,
All the day's rewards waiting at the doors of sleep . . .

MORNING, NOON, AND NIGHT

I

And the morning green, and the buildup of weather, and my brows
Have not been brushed, and never will be, by the breezes of divinity.
That much is clear, at least to me, but yesterday I noticed
Something floating in and out of clouds, something like a bird,
But also like a man, black-suited, with his arms outspread.
And I thought this could be a sign that I've been wrong. Then I woke,
And on my bed the shadow of the future fell, and on the liquid ruins
Of the sea outside, and on the shells of buildings at the water's edge.
A rapid overcast blew in, bending trees and flattening fields. I stayed
    in bed,
Hoping it would pass. What might have been still waited for its
    chance.

II

Whatever the star charts told us to watch for or the maps
Said we would find, nothing prepared us for what we discovered.
We toiled away in the shadowless depths of noon,
While an alien wind slept in the branches, and dead leaves
Turned to dust in the streets. Cities of light, long summers
Of leisure were not to be ours; for to come as we had, long after
It mattered, to live among tombs, great as they are,
Was to be no nearer the end, no farther from where we began.

III

These nights of pinks and purples vanishing, of freakish heat
That strokes our skin until we fall asleep and stray to places
We hoped would always be beyond our reach—the deeps
Where nothing flourishes, where everything that happens seems
To be for keeps. We sweat, and plead to be released
Into the coming day on time, and panic at the thought
Of never getting there and being forced to drift forgotten
On a midnight sea where every thousand years a ship is sighted, or a
    swan,
Or a drowned swimmer whose imagination has outlived his fate, and
    who swims
To prove, to no one in particular, how false his life had been.

A PIECE OF THE STORM

for Sharon Horvath

From the shadow of domes in the city of domes,
A snowflake, a blizzard of one, weightless, entered your room
And made its way to the arm of the chair where you, looking up
From your book, saw it the moment it landed. That's all
There was to it. No more than a solemn waking
To brevity, to the lifting and falling away of attention, swiftly,
A time between times, a flowerless funeral. No more than that
Except for the feeling that this piece of the storm,
Which turned into nothing before your eyes, would come back,
That someone years hence, sitting as you are now, might say:
"It's time. The air is ready. The sky has an opening."

A SUITE OF APPEARANCES

for Octavio and Marie Jo Paz

I

Out of what dark or lack has he come to wait
At the edge of your gaze for the moment when you
Would look up and see through the trembling leaves

His shadow suddenly there? Out of what place has he come
To enter the light that remains, and say in the weightless
Cadence of those who arrive from a distance that the crossing

Was hard with only a gleam to follow over the Sea of Something,
Which opens and closes, breaks and flashes, spreading its cold,
Watery foliage wherever it can to catch you and carry you

And leave you where you have never been, that he has escaped
To tell you with all that is left of his voice that this is his
Story, which continues wherever the end is happening?

II

No wonder—since things come into view then drop from sight—
We clear a space for ourselves, a stillness where nothing
Is blurred: a common palm, an oasis in which to rest, to sit

For hours beside the pool while the moonlight builds its palaces,
And columns rise, and coral chambers open onto patios
With songbirds practicing their peeps and trills.

No wonder the evening paper lies unread, no wonder what happened
Before tonight, the history of ourselves, leaves us cold.

III

How it comes forward, and deposits itself like wind
In the ear which hears only the humming at first, the first
Suggestion of what is to come, how it grows out of itself,

Out of the humming because if it didn't it would die
In the graveyard of sound without being known, and then
Nothing would happen for days or weeks until something like it

Came back, a sound announcing itself as your own, a voice
That is yours, bending under the weight of desire,
Suddenly turning your language into a field unfolding

And all the while the humming can still be detected, the original
Humming before it was yours, and you lie back and hear it,
Surprised that what you are saying was something you meant,

And you think that perhaps you are not who you thought, that
    henceforth
Any idea of yourself must include a body surrounding a song.

IV

In another time, we will want to know how the earth looked
Then, and were people the way we are now. In another time,
The records they left will convince us that we are unchanged

And could be at ease in the past, and not alone in the present.
And we shall be pleased. But beyond all that, what cannot
Be seen or explained will always be elsewhere, always supposed,

Invisible even beneath the signs—the beautiful surface,
The uncommon knowledge—that point its way. In another time,
What cannot be seen will define us, and we shall be prompted

To say that language is error, and all things are wronged
By representation. The self, we shall say, can never be
Seen with a disguise, and never be seen without one.

V

To sit in this chair and wonder where is endlessness
Born, where does it go, how close has it come; and to see
The snow coming down, the flakes enlarging whatever they touch,

Changing shapes until no shape remains. In their descent
They are like stars overtaken by light, or like thoughts
That drift before the long, blank windows facing the future,

Withering, whirling, continuing down, finally away
From the clear panes into the place where nothing will do,
Where nothing is needed or said because it is already known.

And when it is over, and the deep, unspeakable reaches of white
Melt into memory, how will the warmth of the fire,
So long in coming, keep us from mourning the loss?

VI

Of occasions flounced with rose and gold in which the sun
Sinks deep and drowns in a blackening sea, of those, and more,
To be tired. To have the whole sunset again, moment by moment,

As it occurred, in a correct and detailed account, only darkens
Our sense of what happened. There is a limit to what we can picture
And to how much of a good thing is a good thing. Better to hope

For the merest reminder, a spectral glimpse—there but not there,
Something not quite a scene, poised only to be dissolved,
So, when it goes as it must, no sense of loss springs in its wake.

The houses, the gardens, the roaming dogs, let them become
The factors of absence, an incantation of the ineffable.
The backyard was red, that much we know. And the church bell

Tolled the hour. What more is there? The odors of food,
The last traces of dinner, are gone. The glasses are washed.
The neighborhood sleeps. Will the same day ever come back, and with it

Our amazement at having been in it, or will only a dark haze
Spread at the back of the mind, erasing events, one after
The other, so brief they may have been lost to begin with?

HERE

The sun that silvers all the buildings here
Has slid behind a cloud, and left the once bright air
Something less than blue. Yet everything is clear.
Across the road, some dead plants dangle down from rooms
Unoccupied for months, two empty streets converge
On a central square, and on a nearby hill some tombs,
Half buried in a drift of wild grass, appear to merge
With houses at the edge of town. A breeze
Stirs up some dust, turns up a page or two, then dies.
All the boulevards are lined with leafless trees.
There are no dogs nosing around, no birds, no buzzing flies.
Dust gathers everywhere—on stools and bottles in the bars,
On shelves and racks of clothing in department stores,
On the blistered dashboards of abandoned cars.
Within the church, whose massive, rotting doors
Stay open, it is cool, so if a visitor should wander in
He could easily relax, kneel and pray,
Or watch the dirty light pour through the baldachin,
Or think about the heat outside that does not go away,
Which might be why there are no people there—who knows—
Or about the dragon that he saw when he arrived,
Curled up before its cave in saurian repose,
And about how good it is to be survived.

TWO DE CHIRICOS

for Harry Ford

1. THE PHILOSOPHER'S CONQUEST

This melancholy moment will remain,
So, too, the oracle beyond the gate,
And always the tower, the boat, the distant train.

Somewhere to the south a duke is slain,
A war is won. Here, it is too late.
This melancholy moment will remain.

Here, an autumn evening without rain,
Two artichokes abandoned on a crate,
And always the tower, the boat, the distant train.

Is this another scene of childhood pain?
Why do the clock hands say 1:28?
This melancholy moment will remain.

The green and yellow light of love's domain
Falls upon the joylessness of fate,
And always the tower, the boat, the distant train.

The things our vision wills us to contain,
The life of objects, their unbearable weight.
This melancholy moment will remain,
And always the tower, the boat, the distant train.

2. THE DISQUIETING MUSES

Boredom sets in first, and then despair.
One tries to brush it off. It only grows.
Something about the silence of the square.

Something is wrong; something about the air,
Its color; about the light, the way it glows.
Boredom sets in first, and then despair.

The muses in their fluted evening wear,
Their faces blank, might lead one to suppose
Something about the silence of the square,

Something about the buildings standing there.
But no, they have no purpose but to pose.
Boredom sets in first, and then despair.

What happens after that, one doesn't care.
What brought one here—the desire to compose
Something about the silence of the square,

Or something else, of which one's not aware,
Life itself, perhaps—who really knows?
Boredom sets in first, and then despair . . .
Something about the silence of the square.

SOME LAST WORDS

1

It is easier for a needle to pass through a camel
Than for a poor man to enter a woman of means.
Just go to the graveyard and ask around.

2

Eventually, you slip outside, letting the door
Bang shut on your latest thought. What was it anyway?
Just go to the graveyard and ask around.

3

"Negligence" is the perfume I love.
O Fedora. Fedora. If you want any,
Just go to the graveyard and ask around.

4

The bones of the buffalo, the rabbit at sunset,
The wind and its double, the tree, the town . . .
Just go to the graveyard and ask around.

5

If you think good things are on their way
And the world will improve, don't hold your breath.
Just go to the graveyard and ask around.

6

You over there, why do you ask if this is the valley
Of limitless blue, and if we are its prisoners?
Just go to the graveyard and ask around.

7

Life is a dream that is never recalled when the sleeper awakes.
If this is beyond you, Magnificent One,
Just go to the graveyard and ask around.

III

FIVE DOGS

1

I, the dog they call Spot, was about to sing. Autumn
Had come, the walks were freckled with leaves, and a tarnished
Moonlit emptiness crept over the valley floor.
I wanted to climb the poets' hill before the winter settled in;
I wanted to praise the soul. My neighbor told me
Not to waste my time. Already the frost had deepened
And the north wind, trailing the whip of its own scream,
Pressed against the house. "A dog's sublimity is never news,"
He said, "what's another poet in the end?"
And I stood in the midnight valley, watching the great star fields
Flash and flower in the wished-for reaches of heaven.
That's when I, the dog they call Spot, began to sing.

2

Now that the great dog I worshipped for years
Has become none other than myself, I can look within
And bark, and I can look at the mountains down the street
And bark at them as well. I am an eye that sees itself
Look back, a nose that tracks the scent of shadows
As they fall, an ear that picks up sounds
Before they're born. I am the last of the platinum
Retrievers, the end of a gorgeous line.
But there's no comfort being who I am.
I roam around and ponder fate's abolishments
Until my eyes are filled with tears and I say to myself, "Oh Rex,
Forget. Forget. The stars are out. The marble moon slides by."

3

for Neil Welliver

Most of my kind believe that Earth
Is the only planet not covered with hair. So be it,
I say, let tragedy strike, let the story of everything
End today, then let it begin again tomorrow. I no longer care.
I no longer wait in front of the blistered, antique mirror,
Hoping a shape or a self will rise, and step
From that misted surface and say: You there,
Come with me into the world of light and be whole,
For the love you thought had been dead a thousand years
Is back in town and asking for you. Oh no.
I say, I'm done with my kind. I live alone
On Walnut Lane, and will until the day I die.

4

Before the tremendous dogs are unleashed,
Let's get the little ones inside, let's drag
The big bones onto the lawn and clean the Royal Dog Hotel.
Gypsy, my love, the end of an age has come. Already,
The howls of the great dogs practicing fills the air,
And look at that man on all fours dancing under
The moon's dumbfounded gaze, and look at that woman
Doing the same. The wave of the future has gotten
To them and they have responded with all they have:
A little step forward, a little step back. And they sway,
And their eyes are closed. O heavenly bodies.
O bodies of time. O golden bodies of lasting fire.

(AFTER A LINE OF JOHN ASHBERY'S)

5

All winter the weather came up with amazing results:
The streets and walks had turned to glass. The sky
Was a sheet of white. And here was a dog in a phone booth
Calling home. But nothing would ease his tiny heart.
For years the song of his body was all of his calling. Now
It was nothing. Those hymns to desire, songs of bliss
Would never return. The sky's copious indigo,
The yellow dust of sunlight after rain, were gone.
No one was home. The phone kept ringing. The curtains
Of sleep were about to be drawn, and darkness would pass
Into the world. And so, and so . . . goodbye all, goodbye dog.

IV

IN MEMORY OF JOSEPH BRODSKY

It could be said, even here, that what remains of the self
Unwinds into a vanishing light, and thins like dust, and heads
To a place where knowing and nothing pass into each other, and
    through;
That it moves, unwinding still, beyond the vault of brightness ended,
And continues to a place which may never be found, where the
    unsayable,
Finally, once more is uttered, but lightly, quickly, like random rain
That passes in sleep, that one imagines passes in sleep.
What remains of the self unwinds and unwinds, for none
Of the boundaries holds—neither the shapeless one between us,
Nor the one that falls between your body and your voice. Joseph,
Dear Joseph, those sudden reminders of your having been—the places
And times whose greatest life was the one you gave them—now
    appear
Like ghosts in your wake. What remains of the self unwinds
Beyond us, for whom time is only a measure of meanwhile
And the future no more than et cetera et cetera . . . but fast and
    forever.

WHAT IT WAS

I

It was impossible to imagine, impossible
Not to imagine; the blueness of it, the shadow it cast,
Falling downward, filling the dark with the chill of itself,
The cold of it falling out of itself, out of whatever idea
Of itself it described as it fell; a something, a smallness,
A dot, a speck, a speck within a speck, an endless depth
Of smallness; a song, but less than a song, something drowning
Into itself, something going, a flood of sound, but less
Than a sound; the last of it, the blank of it,
The tender small blank of it filling its echo, and falling,
And rising unnoticed, and falling again, and always thus,
And always because, and only because, once having been, it was . . .

II

It was the beginning of a chair;
It was the gray couch; it was the walls,
The garden, the gravel road; it was the way
The ruined moonlight fell across her hair.
It was that, and it was more. It was the wind that tore
At the trees; it was the fuss and clutter of clouds, the shore
Littered with stars. It was the hour which seemed to say
That if you knew what time it really was, you would not
Ask for anything again. It was that. It was certainly that.
It was also what never happened—a moment so full
That when it went, as it had to, no grief was large enough
To contain it. It was the room that appeared unchanged
After so many years. It was that. It was the hat
She'd forgotten to take, the pen she left on the table.
It was the sun on my hand. It was the sun's heat. It was the way
I sat, the way I waited for hours, for days. It was that. Just that.

THE DELIRIUM WALTZ

I cannot remember when it began. The lights were low. We were walking across the floor, over polished wood and inlaid marble, through shallow water, through dustings of snow, through cloudy figures of fallen light. I cannot remember but I think you were there—whoever you were—sometimes with me, sometimes watching. Shapes assembled themselves and dissolved. The hall to the ballroom seemed endless, and a voice—perhaps it was yours—was saying we'd never arrive. Now we were gliding over the floor, our clothes were heavy, the music was slow, and I thought we would die all over again. I believe we were happy. We moved in the drift of sound, and whether we went toward the future or back to the past we weren't able to tell. Anxiety has its inflections—wasteful, sad, tragic at times—but here it had none. In its harmless hovering it was merely fantastic, so we kept dancing. I think I was leading. Why else would I practice those near calamitous dips? I think it was clear that we had always been dancing, always been eager to give ourselves to the rapture of music. Even the simplest movement, from the wafting of clouds to the wink of an eye, could catch and hold our attention. The rooms became larger and finally dimensionless, and we kept gliding, gliding and turning.

And then came Bob and Sonia
And the dance was slow
And joining them now were Chip and Molly
And Joseph dear Joseph was dancing and smoking

And the dance was slow
And into the hall years later came Tom and Em
And Joseph dear Joseph was dancing and smoking
And Bill and Sandy were leaning together

And into the hall years later came Tom and Em
Holding each other and turning and turning
And Bill and Sandy were leaning together
And Wally and Deb and Jorie and Jim

Holding each other and turning and turning
Then came Jules tall and thin
And Wally and Deb and Jorie and Jim
Everyone moving everyone dancing

Then came Jules tall and thin
Across the wide floor
Everyone moving everyone dancing
Harry was there and so was Kathleen

Across the wide floor
Looking better than ever came Jessie and Steve
Harry was there and so was Kathleen
And Peter and Barbara had just gotten back

Looking better than ever came Jessie and Steve
Leon and Judith Muffie and Jim
And Peter and Barbara had just gotten back
And others were there

Leon and Judith Muffie and Jim
Charlie and Helen were eating and dancing
And others were there
Wearing their best

Charlie and Helen were eating and dancing
Glenn and Angela Buck and Cathy
Wearing their best
Around and around dancing and dancing

And our shadows floated away toward sunset and darkened the backs of birds, and blackened the sea whose breath smelled slightly of fish, of almonds, of rotting fruit. Soon the air was soiled with dust and purple clouds. We were standing, watching everyone else afloat on the floor, on the sea of the floor, like a raft of voices. "Hello," they said, as they sailed by, "may we have this dance?" And off they went to another room with pale blue walls and birds.

And one room led to another
And birds flew back and forth
People roamed the veranda
Under the limbs of trees

And birds flew back and forth
A golden haze was everywhere
Under the limbs of trees
And Howie was there with Francine

A golden haze was everywhere
And Jeannette and Buddy were dancing
And Howie was there with Francine
Angels must always be pale they said

And Jeannette and Buddy were dancing
And Louise and Karen were talking
Angels must always be pale they said
But pale turns round to white

And Louise and Karen were talking
Saying that blue slides into black
But pale turns round to white
And Jules was there in heels

Saying that blue slides into black
Rosanna was there and Maria
And Jules was there in heels
And day and night were one

Rosanna was there and Maria
And Rusty and Carol were there
And day and night were one
And the sea's green body was near

And Rusty and Carol were there
And Charles and Holly were dancing
And the sea's green body was near
Hello out there hello

And Charles and Holly were dancing
So thin they were and light
Hello out there hello
Can anyone hear out there

And the rush of water was loud as if the ballroom were flooded. And I was dancing alone in the absence of all that I knew and was bound by. And here was the sea—the blur, the erasure of difference, the end of self, the end of whatever surrounds the self. And I kept going. The breakers flashed and fell under the moon's gaze. Scattered petals of foam shone briefly, then sank in the sand. It was cold, and I found myself suddenly back with the others. That vast ungraspable body, the sea, that huge and meaningless empire of water, was left on its own.

They drifted over the floor
And the silver sparkled a little
Oh how they moved together
The crystals shook in the draft

And the silver sparkled a little
So many doors were open
The crystals shook in the draft
Nobody knew what would happen

So many doors were open
And there was Eleanor dancing
Nobody knew what would happen
Now Red waltzed into the room

And there was Eleanor dancing
And Don and Jean were waiting
Now Red waltzed into the room
The years would come and go

And Don and Jean were waiting
Hours and hours would pass
The years would come and go
The palms in the hallway rustled

Hours and hours would pass
Now enter the children of Em
The palms in the hallway rustled
And here were the children of Tom

Now enter the children of Em
There was nothing to do but dance
And here were the children of Tom
And Nolan was telling them something

There was nothing to do but dance
They would never sit down together
And Nolan was telling them something
And many who wished they could

Would never sit down together
The season of dancing was endless
And many who wished they could
Would never be able to stop

I cannot remember when it began. The lights were low. We were walking across the floor, over polished wood and inlaid marble, through shallow water, through dustings of snow, through cloudy figures of fallen light. I cannot remember, but I think you were there, whoever you were.

THE VIEW

for Derek Walcott

This is the place. The chairs are white. The table shines.
The person sitting there stares at the waxen glow.
The wind moves the air around, repeatedly,
As if to clear a space. "A space for me," he thinks.
He's always been drawn to the weather of leavetaking,
Arranging itself so that grief—even the most intimate—
Might be read from a distance. A long shelf of cloud
Hangs above the open sea with the sun, the sun
Of no distinction, sinking behind it—a mild version
Of the story that is told just once if true, and always too late.
The waitress brings his drink, which he holds
Against the waning light, but just for a moment.
Its red reflection tints his shirt. Slowly the sky becomes darker,
The wind relents, the view sublimes. The violet sweep of it
Seems, in this effortless nightfall, more than a reason
For being there, for seeing it, seems itself a kind
Of happiness, as if that plain fact were enough and would last.

MAN AND CAMEL

One

THE KING

I went to the middle of the room and called out,
"I know you're here," then noticed him in the corner,
looking tiny in his jeweled crown and his cape
with ermine trim. "I have lost my desire to rule,"
he said. "My kingdom is empty except for you,
and all you do is ask for me." "But Your Majesty—"
"Don't 'Your Majesty' me," he said, and tilted his head
to one side and closed his eyes. "There," he whispered,
"that's more like it," and he entered his dream
like a mouse vanishing into its hole.

I HAD BEEN A POLAR EXPLORER

I had been a polar explorer in my youth
and spent countless days and nights freezing
in one blank place and then another. Eventually,
I quit my travels and stayed at home,
and there grew within me a sudden excess of desire,
as if a brilliant stream of light of the sort one sees
within a diamond were passing through me.
I filled page after page with visions of what I had witnessed—
groaning seas of pack ice, giant glaciers, and the windswept white
of icebergs. Then, with nothing more to say, I stopped
and turned my sights on what was near. Almost at once,
a man wearing a dark coat and broad-brimmed hat
appeared under the trees in front of my house.
The way he stared straight ahead and stood,
not shifting his weight, letting his arms hang down
at his sides, made me think that I knew him.
But when I raised my hand to say hello,
he took a step back, turned away, and started to fade
as longing fades until nothing is left of it.

TWO HORSES

On a warm night in June
I went to the lake, got on all fours,
and drank like an animal. Two horses
came up beside me to drink as well.
"This is amazing," I thought, "but who will believe it?"
The horses eyed me from time to time, snorting
and nodding. I felt the need to respond, so I snorted, too,
but haltingly, as though not really wanting to be heard.
The horses must have sensed that I was holding back.
They moved slightly away. Then I thought they might have known me
in another life—the one in which I was a poet.
They might have even read my poems, for back then,
in that shadowy time when our eagerness knew no bounds,
we changed styles almost as often as there were days in the year.

I am not thinking of Death, but Death is thinking of me.
He leans back in his chair, rubs his hands, strokes
his beard, and says, "I'm thinking of Strand, I'm thinking
that one of these days I'll be out back, swinging my scythe
or holding my hourglass up to the moon, and Strand will appear
in a jacket and tie, and together under the boulevards'
leafless trees we'll stroll into the city of souls. And when
we get to the Great Piazza with its marble mansions, the crowd
that had been waiting there will welcome us with delirious cries,
and their tears, turned hard and cold as glass from having been
held back so long, will fall and clatter on the stones below.
        O let it be soon. Let it be soon."

MAN AND CAMEL

On the eve of my fortieth birthday
I sat on the porch having a smoke
when out of the blue a man and a camel
happened by. Neither uttered a sound
at first, but as they drifted up the street
and out of town the two of them began to sing.
Yet what they sang is still a mystery to me—
the words were indistinct and the tune
too ornamental to recall. Into the desert
they went and as they went their voices
rose as one above the sifting sound
of windblown sand. The wonder of their singing,
its elusive blend of man and camel, seemed
an ideal image for all uncommon couples.
Was this the night that I had waited for
so long? I wanted to believe it was,
but just as they were vanishing, the man
and camel ceased to sing, and galloped
back to town. They stood before my porch,
staring up at me with beady eyes, and said:
"You ruined it. You ruined it forever."

ERROR

We drifted downstream under a scattering of stars
and slept until the sun rose. When we got to the capital,
which lay in ruins, we built a large fire out of what chairs
and tables we could find. The heat was so fierce that birds
overhead caught fire and fell flaming to earth.
These we ate, then continued on foot into regions
where the sea is frozen and the ground is strewn
with moonlike boulders. If only we had stopped,
turned, and gone back to the garden we started from,
with its broken urn, its pile of rotting leaves, and sat
gazing up at the house and seen only the passing
of sunlight over its windows, that would have been
enough, even if the wind cried and clouds scudded seaward
like the pages of a book on which nothing was written.

FIRE

Sometimes there would be a fire and I would walk into it
and come out unharmed and continue on my way,
and for me it was just another thing to have done.
As for putting out the fire, I left that to others
who would rush into the billowing smoke with brooms
and blankets to smother the flames. When they were through
they would huddle together to talk of what they had seen—
how lucky they were to have witnessed the lusters of heat,
the hushing effect of ashes, but even more to have known the
    fragrance
of burning paper, the sound of words breathing their last.

CAKE

A man leaves for the next town to pick up a cake.
On the way, he gets lost in a dense woods
and the cake is never picked up. Years later,
the man appears on a beach, staring at the sea.
"I am standing on a beach," he thinks, "and I am lost
in thought." He does not move. The heaving sea
turns black, its waves curl and crash. "Soon
I will leave," he continues. "Soon I will go
to a nearby town to pick up a cake. I will walk
in a brown and endless woods, and far away
the heaving sea will turn to black, and the waves—
I can see them now—will curl and crash."

THE ROSE

The sorrows of the rose were mounting up.
Twisted in a field of weeds, the helpless rose
felt the breeze of paradise just once, then died.
The children cried, "Oh rose, come back.
We love you, rose." Then someone said that soon
they'd have another rose. "Come, my darlings,
down to the pond, lean over the edge and look
at yourselves looking up. Now do you see it,
its petals open, rising to the surface, turning into you?"
"Oh no," they said. "We are what we are—nothing else."

How perfect. How ancient. How past repair.

2032

It is evening in the town of X
where Death, who used to love me, sits
in a limo with a blanket spread across his thighs,
waiting for his driver to appear. His hair
is white, his eyes have gotten small, his cheeks
have lost their luster. He has not swung his scythe
in years, or touched his hourglass. He is waiting
to be driven to the Blue Hotel, the ultimate resort,
where an endless silence fills the lilac-scented air,
and marble fish swim motionless in marble seas,
and where . . . Where is his driver? Ah, there she is,
coming down the garden steps, in heels, velvet evening gown,
and golden boa, blowing kisses to the trees.

STORM

On the last night of our house arrest
a howling wind tore through the streets,
ripping down shutters, scattering roof tiles,
leaving behind a river of refuse. When the sun
rose over the marble gate, I could see the guards,
sluggish in the morning heat, desert their posts
and stagger toward the woods just out of town.
"Darling," I said, "let's go, the guards have left,
the place is a ruin." But she was oblivious.
"You go," she said, and she pulled up the sheet
to cover her eyes. I ran downstairs and called
for my horse. "To the sea," I whispered, and off
we went and how quick we were, my horse and I,
riding over the fresh green fields, as if to our freedom.

CONVERSATION

1

He said it would always be what might have been,
a city about to happen, a city never completed,
one that disappeared with hardly a trace, inside
or beneath the outer city, making the outer one—
the one in which we spend our waking hours—
seem pointless and dull. It would always be
a city in the dark, a city so shy that it waited,
dreading the moment that was never to be.

2

I said that the dawning of the unknown
was always before us and that the realization
of anything is a constant threat. I also said
that there is sadness in knowing that the undoing
of what has been done will never take place,
that the history of now is as distant as the future
of when. Our skills are limited, our power
to imagine enfeebled, our cities doomed.
All roads lead to the malodorous sea.

AFTERWORDS

1

Packs of wild dogs roamed the streets of the very rich,
looking for scraps that might have been thrown their way
by a caring cook or merciful maid. Birds flew in
from everywhere, going up and down and side to side.
In the distance, beyond the stucco mansions
with their patios and pools, beyond the cemetery
with its marble angels, barely visible to the naked eye,
a man was scaling a cliff, then stopped and turned, and
opened his mouth to scream, but when the screams arrived
they were faint and cold, no different from the snow
that kept on falling through the windless night.

2

They rushed from their houses to welcome the spring,
then ran to the piers to gaze at the backs of fish,
long and glistening, then to the stables to see
the sleek, cloud-breathing horses. Nothing could keep them
from their joy, neither the storm gathering strength
in the west nor the bombs going off in the east;
theirs was the bliss of another age. Suddenly,
a woman appeared on the beach and said that soon
she would sing. "Soon she will sing," murmured
the gathering crowd. "Soon she will sing," I said
to myself as I woke. Then I went to the window
and a river of old people with canes and flashlights
were inching their way down through the dark to the sea.

3

Twenty crows sat on the limbs of an elm.
The air was so clear that one could see up
the broad valley of patchwork fields to the next town
where a train releasing a ribbon of steam
pulled out of a small wood station. Minutes later,
a man stepped onto the platform, waited, then lifted
his suitcase over his head and hurled it onto the tracks.
"That's that," he said, and turned and walked away.
The crows had taken off, it was cold, and up ahead
long, windblown shadows lashed the passive ground.

ELEVATOR

1

The elevator went to the basement. The doors opened.
A man stepped in and asked if I was going up.
"I'm going down," I said. "I won't be going up."

2

The elevator went to the basement. The doors opened.
A man stepped in and asked if I was going up.
"I'm going down," I said. "I won't be going up."

Two

BLACK SEA

One clear night while the others slept, I climbed
the stairs to the roof of the house and under a sky
strewn with stars I gazed at the sea, at the spread of it,
the rolling crests of it raked by the wind, becoming
like bits of lace tossed in the air. I stood in the long,
whispering night, waiting for something, a sign, the approach
of a distant light, and I imagined you coming closer,
the dark waves of your hair mingling with the sea,
and the dark became desire, and desire the arriving light.
The nearness, the momentary warmth of you as I stood
on that lonely height watching the slow swells of the sea
break on the shore and turn briefly into glass and disappear . . .
Why did I believe you would come out of nowhere? Why with all
that the world offers would you come only because I was here?

MOTHER AND SON

The son enters the mother's room
and stands by the bed where the mother lies.
The son believes that she wants to tell him
what he longs to hear—that he is her boy,
always her boy. The son leans down to kiss
the mother's lips, but her lips are cold.
The burial of feelings has begun. The son
touches the mother's hands one last time,
then turns and sees the moon's full face.
An ashen light falls across the floor.
If the moon could speak, what would it say?
If the moon could speak, it would say nothing.

MIRROR

A white room and a party going on
and I was standing with some friends
under a large gilt-framed mirror
that tilted slightly forward
over the fireplace.
We were drinking whiskey
and some of us, feeling no pain,
were trying to decide
what precise shade of yellow
the setting sun turned our drinks.
I closed my eyes briefly,
then looked up into the mirror:
a woman in a green dress leaned
against the far wall.
She seemed distracted,
the fingers of one hand
fidgeted with her necklace,
and she was staring into the mirror,
not at me, but past me, into a space
that might be filled by someone
yet to arrive, who at that moment
could be starting the journey
which would lead eventually to her.
Then, suddenly, my friends
said it was time to move on.
This was years ago,
and though I have forgotten
where we went and who we all were,
I still recall that moment of looking up

and seeing the woman stare past me
into a place I could only imagine,
and each time it is with a pang,
as if just then I were stepping
from the depths of the mirror
into that white room, breathless and eager,
only to discover too late
that she is not there.

MOON

Open the book of evening to the page
where the moon, always the moon, appears

between two clouds, moving so slowly that hours
will seem to have passed before you reach the next page

where the moon, now brighter, lowers a path
to lead you away from what you have known

into those places where what you had wished for happens,
its lone syllable like a sentence poised

at the edge of sense, waiting for you to say its name
once more as you lift your eyes from the page

and close the book, still feeling what it was like
to dwell in that light, that sudden paradise of sound.

PEOPLE WALKING THROUGH THE NIGHT

They carried what they had in garbage bags and knapsacks,
long lines of them winding down country roads, through barren
fields to the edge of town, then onto numbered streets, by rows
of leafless trees and heaps of rubble. When they reached
the central square, they covered themselves with blankets
and pieces of cardboard, and slept on benches or leaned
on broken slabs of concrete, smoking, watching the faint
gray flags of their breath being lifted away, the swift moon
climbing the sky, their thin dogs searching for carrion.

MARSYAS

Something was wrong
Screams could be heard
In the morning dark
It was cold

Screams could be heard
A storm was coming
It was cold
And the screams were piercing

A storm was coming
Someone was struggling
And the screams were piercing
Hard to imagine

Someone was struggling
So close, so close
Hard to imagine
A man was tearing open his body

So close, so close
The screams were unbearable
A man was tearing open his body
What could we do

The screams were unbearable
His flesh was in ribbons
What could we do
The rain came down

His flesh was in ribbons
And nobody spoke
The rain came down
There were flashes of lightning

And nobody spoke
Trees shook in the wind
There were flashes of lightning
Then came thunder

THE WEBERN VARIATIONS

The sudden rush of it
pushing aside the branches,
late summer flashing toward
the image of its absence

*

Into the heart of nothing,
into the radiant hollows,
even the language of vanishing
leaves itself behind

*

Clouds, trees, houses,
in the feeling they awaken
as the dark approaches, seem
like pieces of another life

*

One can sift through what remains—
the dust of phrases uttered once,
the ruins of a passion—
it comes to less each time

*

The voice sliding down,
the voice turning round
and lengthening the thread
of sense, the thread of sound

*

Those avenues of light
that slid between the clouds
moments ago are gone,
and suddenly it is dark

*

Who will be left to stitch
and sew the shroud of song,
the houses back in place, the trees
rising from a purple shade?

*

Not too late to see oneself
walk the beach at night,
how easily the sea comes in,
spreads, retreats, and disappears

*

How easily it breathes,
and the late-risen half-moon,
drawn out of darkness, staring down,
seems to pause above the waves

*

Under the moon and stars,
which are what they have always been,
what should we be but ourselves
in this light, which is no light to speak of?

*

What should we hear but the voice
that would be ours shaping itself,
the secret voice of being telling us
that where we disappear is where we are?

*

What to make of a season's end,
the drift of cold drawn down
the hallways of the night,
the wind pushing aside the leaves?

*

The vision of one's passing passes,
days flow into other days,
the voice that sews and stitches
again picks up its work

*

And everything turns and turns
and the unknown turns into the song
that is the known, but what in turn
becomes of the song is not for us to say

MY NAME

Once when the lawn was a golden green
and the marbled moonlit trees rose like fresh memorials
in the scented air, and the whole countryside pulsed
with the chirr and murmur of insects, I lay in the grass,
feeling the great distances open above me, and wondered
what I would become and where I would find myself,
and though I barely existed, I felt for an instant
that the vast star-clustered sky was mine, and I heard
my name as if for the first time, heard it the way
one hears the wind or the rain, but faint and far off
as though it belonged not to me but to the silence
from which it had come and to which it would go.

Three

POEM AFTER THE SEVEN LAST WORDS

1

The story of the end, of the last word
of the end, when told, is a story that never ends.
We tell it and retell it—one word, then another
until it seems that no last word is possible,
that none would be bearable. Thus, when the hero
of the story says to himself, as to someone far away,
"Forgive them, for they know not what they do,"
we may feel that he is pleading for us, that we are
the secret life of the story and, as long as his plea
is not answered, we shall be spared. So the story
continues. So we continue. And the end, once more,
becomes the next, and the next after that.

There is an island in the dark, a dreamt-of place
where the muttering wind shifts over the white lawns
and riffles the leaves of trees, the high trees
that are streaked with gold and line the walkways there;
and those already arrived are happy to be the silken
remains of something they were but cannot recall;
they move to the sound of stars, which is also imagined,
but who cares about that; the polished columns they see
may be no more than shafts of sunlight, but for those
who live on and on in the radiance of their remains
this is of little importance. There is an island
in the dark and you will be there, I promise you, you
shall be with me in paradise, in the single season of being,
in the place of forever, you shall find yourself. And there
the leaves will turn and never fall, there the wind
will sing and be your voice as if for the first time.

3

Someday someone will write a story telling
among other things of a parting between mother
and son, of how she wandered off, of how he vanished
in air. But before that happens, it will describe
how their faces shone with a feeble light and how
the son was moved to say, "Woman, look at your son,"
then to a friend nearby, "Son, look at your mother."
At which point the writer will put down his pen
and imagine that while those words were spoken
something else happened, something unusual like
a purpose revealed, a secret exchanged, a truth
to which they, the mother and son, would be bound,
but what it was no one would know. Not even the writer.

4

These are the days of spring when the sky is filled
with the odor of lilac, when darkness becomes desire,
and there is nothing that does not wish to be born;
days when the fate of the present is a breezy fullness,
when the world's great gift for fiction gilds even
the dirt we walk on, and we feel we could live forever
while knowing of course that we can't. Such is our plight.
The master of weather and everything else, if he wants,
can bring forth a dark of a different kind, one hidden
by darkness so deep it cannot be seen. No one escapes.
Not even the man who believed he was chosen to do so,
for when the dark came down he cried out, "Father, Father,
why have you forsaken me?" To which no answer came.

5

To be thirsty. To say, "I thirst."
To close one's eyes and see the giant world
that is born each time the eyes are closed.
To see one's death. To see the darkening clouds
as the tragic cloth of a day of mourning. To be the one
mourned. To open the dictionary of the Beyond and discover
what one suspected, that the only word in it
is nothing. To try to open one's eyes, but not to be
able to. To feel the mouth burn. To feel the sudden
presence of what, again and again, was not said.
To translate it and have it remain unsaid. To know
at last that nothing is more real than nothing.

6

"It is finished," he said. You could hear him say it,
the words almost a whisper, then not even that,
but an echo so faint it seemed no longer to come
from him, but from elsewhere. This was his moment,
his final moment. "It is finished," he said into a vastness
that led to an even greater vastness, and yet all of it
within him. He contained it all. That was the miracle,
to be both large and small in the same instant, to be
like us, but more so, then finally to give up the ghost,
which is what happened. And from the storm that swirled
in his wake a formal nakedness took shape, the truth
of disguise and the mask of belief were joined forever.

7

Back down these stairs to the same scene,
to the moon, the stars, the night wind. Hours pass
and only the harp off in the distance and the wind
moving through it. And soon the sun's gray disk,
darkened by clouds, sailing above. And beyond,
as always, the sea of endless transparence, of utmost
calm, a place of constant beginning that has within it
what no eye has seen, what no ear has heard, what no hand
has touched, what has not arisen in the human heart.
To that place, to the keeper of that place, I commit myself.

ALMOST INVISIBLE

A BANKER IN THE BROTHEL OF BLIND WOMEN

A banker strutted into the brothel of blind women. "I am a shepherd," he announced, "and blow my shepherd's pipe as often as I can, but I have lost my flock and feel that I am at a critical point in my life." "I can tell by the way you talk," said one of the women, "that you are a banker only pretending to be a shepherd and that you want us to pity you, which we do because you have stooped so low as to try to make fools of us." "My dear," said the banker to the same woman, "I can tell that you are a rich widow looking for a little excitement and are not blind at all." "This observation suggests," said the woman, "that you may be a shepherd after all, for what kind of rich widow would find excitement being a whore only to end up with a banker?" "Exactly," said the banker.

BURY YOUR FACE IN YOUR HANDS

Because we have crossed the river and the wind offers only a numb uncoiling of cold and we have meekly adapted, no longer expecting more than we have been given, nor wondering how it happened that we came to this place, we don't mind that nothing turned out as we thought it might. There is no way to clear the haze in which we live, no way to know that we have undergone another day. The silent snow of thought melts before it has a chance to stick. Where we are is anyone's guess. The gates to nowhere multiply and the present is so far away, so deeply far away.

ANYWHERE COULD BE SOMEWHERE

I might have come from the high country, or maybe the low country, I don't recall which. I might have come from the city, but what city in what country is beyond me. I might have come from the outskirts of a city from which others have come or maybe a city from which only I have come. Who's to know? Who's to decide if it rained or the sun was out? Who's to remember? They say things are happening at the border, but nobody knows which border. They talk of a hotel there, where it doesn't matter if you forgot your suitcase, another will be waiting, big enough, and just for you.

HARMONY IN THE BOUDOIR

After years of marriage, he stands at the foot of the bed and tells his wife that she will never know him, that for everything he says there is more that he does not say, that behind each word he utters there is another word, and hundreds more behind that one. All those unsaid words, he says, contain his true self, which has been betrayed by the superficial self before her. "So you see," he says, kicking off his slippers, "I am more than what I have led you to believe I am." "Oh, you silly man," says his wife, "of course you are. I find that just thinking of you having so many selves receding into nothingness is very exciting. That you barely exist as you are couldn't please me more."

CLARITIES OF THE NONEXISTENT

To have loved the way it happens in the empty hours of late afternoon; to lean back and conceive of a journey leaving behind no trace of itself; to look out from the house and see a figure leaning forward as if into the wind although there is no wind; to see the hats of those in town, discarded in moments of passion, scattered over the ground although one cannot see the ground. All this in the vague, yellowing light that lowers itself in the hour before dark; none of it of value except for the pleasure it gives, enlarging an instant and finally making it seem as if it were true. And years later to come upon the same scene—the figure leaning into the same wind, the same hats scattered over the same ground that one cannot see.

THE MINISTER OF CULTURE GETS HIS WISH

The Minister of Culture goes home after a grueling day at the office. He lies on his bed and tries to think of nothing, but nothing happens or, more precisely, does not happen. Nothing is elsewhere doing what nothing does, which is to expand the dark. But the minister is patient, and slowly things slip away—the walls of his house, the park across the street, his friends in the next town. He believes that nothing has finally come to him and, in its absent way, is saying, "Darling, you know how much I have always wanted to please you, and now I have come. And what is more, I have come to stay."

THE OLD AGE OF NOSTALGIA

Those hours given over to basking in the glow of an imagined future, of being carried away in streams of promise by a love or a passion so strong that one felt altered forever and convinced that even the smallest particle of the surrounding world was charged with a purpose of impossible grandeur; ah, yes, and one would look up into the trees and be thrilled by the wind-loosened river of pale, gold foliage cascading down and by the high, melodious singing of countless birds; those moments, so many and so long ago, still come back, but briefly, like fireflies in the perfumed heat of a summer night.

DREAM TESTICLES, VANISHED VAGINAS

Horace, the corpse, said, "I kept believing that tomorrow would come and I would get up, put on my socks, my boxer shorts, go to the kitchen, make myself coffee, read the paper, and call some friends. But tomorrow came and I was not in it. Instead, I found myself on a powder-blue sofa in a field of bright grass that rolled on forever." "How awful," said Mildred, who was not yet a corpse, but in close touch with Horace, "how awful to be so far away with nothing to do, and without sex to distract you. I've heard that all vaginas up there, even the most open, honest, and energetic, are shut down, and that all testicles, even the most forthright and gifted, swing dreamily among the clouds like little chandeliers."

THE STUDENTS OF THE INEFFABLE

What I am about to say happened years ago. I had rented a house by the sea. Each night I sat on the porch and wished for some surge of feeling, some firelit stream of sound to lead me away from all that I had known. But one night, I climbed the hill behind the house and looked down on a small dirt road where I was surprised to see long lines of people shuffling into the distance. Their difficult breathing and their coughing were probably caused by the cloud of dust their march had created. "Who are you and why is this happening?" I asked one of them. "We are believers and must keep going," and then he added, "our work is important and concerns the self." "But all your dust is darkening the stars," I said. "Nay, nay," he said, "we are only passing through, the stars will return."

THE EVERYDAY ENCHANTMENT OF MUSIC

A rough sound was polished until it became a smoother sound, which was polished until it became music. Then the music was polished until it became the memory of a night in Venice when tears of the sea fell from the Bridge of Sighs, which in turn was polished until it ceased to be and in its place stood the empty home of a heart in trouble. Then suddenly there was sun and the music came back and traffic was moving and off in the distance, at the edge of the city, a long line of clouds appeared, and there was thunder, which, however menacing, would become music, and the memory of what happened after Venice would begin, and what happened after the home of the troubled heart broke in two would also begin.

THE BURIED MELANCHOLY OF THE POET

One summer when he was still young he stood at the window and wondered where they had gone, those women who sat by the ocean, watching, waiting for something that would never arrive, the wind light against their skin, sending loose strands of hair across their lips. From what season had they fallen, from what idea of grace had they strayed? It was long since he had seen them in their lonely splendor, heavy in their idleness, enacting the sad story of hope abandoned. This was the summer he wandered out into the miraculous night, into the sea of dark, as if for the first time, to shed his own light, but what he shed was the dark, what he found was the night.

EVER SO MANY HUNDRED YEARS HENCE

Down the milky corridors of fog, starless scenery, the rubble of ocean's breath, that lone figure strolling, gathering about him without shame a small flood of damages, concessions to a frailty which was his long before he knew what he must do or what he must be, and now, with his hand outstretched as if to greet the future, he comes close and pours out to me the subtlety of his meaning and I see him, my long-lost uncle, great and golden in the sudden sunlight, who predicted that he would reach over the years and be with me and that I would be waiting.

EXHAUSTION AT SUNSET

The empty heart comes home from a busy day at the office. And what is the empty heart to do but empty itself of emptiness. Sweeping out the unsweepable takes an effort of mind, the fruitless exertion of faculties already burdened. Poor empty heart, old before its time, how it struggles to do what the mind tells it to do. But the struggle comes to nothing. The empty heart cannot do what the mind commands. It sits in the dark, daydreams, and the emptiness grows.

CLEAR IN THE SEPTEMBER LIGHT

A man stands under a tree, looking at a small house not far away. He flaps his arms as if he were a bird, maybe signaling someone we cannot see. He could be yelling, but since we hear nothing, he probably is not. Now the wind sends a shiver through the tree and flattens the grass. The man falls to his knees and pounds the ground with his fists. A dog comes and sits beside him, and the man stands, once again flapping his arms. What he does has nothing to do with me. His desperation is not my desperation. I do not stand under trees and look at small houses. I have no dog.

YOU CAN ALWAYS GET THERE FROM HERE

A traveler returned to the country from which he had started many years before. When he stepped from the boat, he noticed how different everything was. There were once many buildings, but now there were few and each of them needed repair. In the park where he played as a child, dust-filled shafts of sunlight struck the tawny leaves of trees and withered hedges. Empty trash bags littered the grass. The air was heavy. He sat on one of the benches and explained to the woman next to him that he'd been away a long time, then asked her what season had he come back to. She replied that it was the only one left, the one they all had agreed on.

THE GALLOWS IN THE GARDEN

In the garden of the great house they are building an immense gallows. The head of the great house, who wears a dark suit which he believes shows him to great advantage, defends the gallows' size by saying that the executed will thus appear small in death. But his critics, whose taste in clothes can never match his, say that the huge gallows will only signify the importance of the hanged. Nonsense, explains the head of the great house, the gallows are more than the gallows and the hanged are less than the hanged. Anything else is unthinkable.

LOVE SILHOUETTED BY LAMPLIGHT

The arm of smoke, grown thin, reaches across the water and set-
tles briefly on a small house near the woods. A husband and wife,
each with a drink in hand, are sitting inside, arguing about which
of them will die first. "I will," says the husband. "No, I will," says
the wife. Then they say, "Maybe we'll die at the same time." They
cannot believe that they are talking this way, so the wife gets up
and says, "If I were an artist, I would paint a portrait of you." "And
if I were an artist," says the husband, "I would do exactly the same."

THE TRIUMPH OF THE INFINITE

I got up in the night and went to the end of the hall. Over the door in large letters it said, "This is the next life. Please come in." I opened the door. Across the room a bearded man in a pale green suit turned to me and said, "Better get ready, we're taking the long way." "Now I'll wake up," I thought, but I was wrong. We began our journey over golden tundra and patches of ice. Then there was nothing for miles around, and all I could hear was my heart pumping and pumping so hard I thought I would die all over again.

THE MYSTERIOUS ARRIVAL
OF AN UNUSUAL LETTER

It had been a long day at work and a long ride back to the small apartment where I lived. When I got there I flicked on the light and saw on the table an envelope with my name on it. Where was the clock? Where was the calendar? The handwriting was my father's, but he had been dead for forty years. As one might, I began to think that maybe, just maybe, he was alive, living a secret life somewhere nearby. How else to explain the envelope? To steady myself, I sat down, opened it, and pulled out the letter. "Dear Son" was the way it began. "Dear Son" and then nothing.

POEM OF THE SPANISH POET

In a hotel room somewhere in Iowa an American poet, tired of his poems, tired of being an American poet, leans back in his chair and imagines he is a Spanish poet, an old Spanish poet, nearing the end of his life, who walks to the Guadalquivir and watches the ships, gray and ghostly in the twilight, slip downstream. The little waves, approaching the grassy bank where he sits, whisper something he can't quite hear as they curl and fall. Now what does the Spanish poet do? He reaches into his pocket, pulls out a notebook, and writes:

> Black fly, black fly
> Why have you come
>
> Is it my shirt
> My new white shirt
>
> With buttons of bone
> Is it my suit
>
> My dark blue suit
> Is it because
>
> I lie here alone
> Under a willow
>
> Cold as stone
> Black fly, black fly
>
> How good you are
> To come to me now

How good you are
To visit me here

Black fly, black fly
To wish me goodbye

THE ENIGMA OF THE INFINITESIMAL

You've seen them at dusk, walking along the shore, seen them standing in doorways, leaning from windows, or straddling the slow-moving edge of a shadow. Lovers of the in-between, they are neither here nor there, neither in nor out. Poor souls, they are driven to experience the impossible. Even at night, they lie in bed with one eye closed and the other open, hoping to catch the last second of consciousness and the first of sleep, to inhabit that no-man's-land, that beautiful place, to behold as only a god might, the luminous conjunction of nothing and all.

A DREAM OF TRAVEL

Comes down from the mountain the cream-colored horse, comes across dun fields and steps lightly into the house, and stands in the bright living room cloudlike and silent. And now, without warning, the gray arm of the wind takes him away. "I loved that horse," thought the poet. "I could have loved anything, but I loved that horse. With him I could have gone to the sea, the wrinkled, sorrowing sea, and who knows what I could have done there—turned wind into marble, made stars shiver in sunlight."

THE EMERGENCY ROOM AT DUSK

The retired commander was upset. His room in the castle was cold, so was the room across the hall, and all the other rooms as well. He should never have bought this castle when there were so many other, cheaper, warmer castles for sale. But he liked the way this one looked—its stone turrets rising into the winter air, its main gate, even its frozen moat, on which he thought someday he might ice-skate, had a silvery charm. He poured himself a brandy and lit a cigar, and tried to concentrate on other things—his many victories, the bravery of his men—but his thoughts swirled in tiny eddies, settling first here, then there, moving as the wind does from empty town to empty town.

ONCE UPON A COLD NOVEMBER MORNING

I left the sunlit fields of my daily life and went down into the hollow mountain, and there I discovered, in all its chilly glory, the glass castle of my other life. I could see right through it, and beyond, but what could I do with it? It was perfect, irreducible, and worthless except for the fact that it existed.

PROVISIONAL ETERNITY

A man and a woman lay in bed. "Just one more time," said the man, "just one more time." "Why do you keep saying that?" said the woman. "Because I never want it to end," said the man. "What don't you want to end?" said the woman. "This," said the man, "this never wanting it to end."

THE STREET AT THE END OF THE WORLD

"Haven't we been down this street before? I think we have; I think they move it every few years, but it keeps coming back with its ravens and dead branches, its crumbling curbs, its lines of people just stepping from a landscape that goes blank the moment they leave it. And what of the walled city with its circling swallows and the sun setting behind it, haven't we seen that before? And what of the ship about to set off to the isle of black rainbows, and midnight flowers, and the bearded tour guides waving us on?" "Yes, my dear, we have seen that too, but now you must hold my arm and close your eyes."

THE NIETZSCHEAN HOURGLASS,
OR THE FUTURE'S MISFORTUNE

Once, as my thought was being drawn through daylight into the bronze corridors of dusk and thence into the promise of dark, I heard out there the strained voice of the hourglass calling for someone to turn it over and show that the future is just an illusion, that what lay ahead was only the past again and again. I was too young for such an idea, so it came back years later as if to prove its own point.

AN EVENT ABOUT WHICH NO MORE NEED BE SAID

I was riding downtown in a cab with a prince who had consented to be interviewed, but asked that I not mention him or his country by name. He explained that both exist secretly and their business is carried on in silence. He was tall, had a long nose beneath which was tucked a tiny mustache; he wore a pale blue shirt open at the neck and cream-colored pants. "I have no hobbies," he explained. "My one interest is sex. It can be with a man or a woman, old or young, so long as it produces the desired result, which is to remind me of the odor of white truffles or the taste of candied violets in a floating island. Here, let me show you something." When I saw it, saw how big it was, and what he'd done to it, I screamed and leaped from the moving cab.

A SHORT PANEGYRIC

Now that the vegetarian nightmare is over and we are back to our diet of meat and deep in the sway of our dark and beautiful habits and able to speak with calm of having survived, let the breeze of the future touch and retouch our large and hungering bodies. Let us march to market to embrace the butcher and put the year of the carrot, the month of the onion behind us, let us worship the roast or the stew that takes its place once again at the sacred center of the dining room table.

HERMETIC MELANCHOLY

Let's say that night has come and the wind has died down and the blue-green trees have turned to gray and the ice mountains, slick under the scarred face of the moon, are like ghosts, motionless in the distance, and the moon's weak light streams into the room where you sit at a table, staring into a glass of whiskey, and where you have been so long that the night, so still, so stark, has become not only your day but the whole of your life; and let's say that while you are there the sun, the actual sun, has risen, and it occurs to you that what you made of the night was only a possibility, a painless, rarified form of despair that could lead, if continued, to an unwanted conclusion, and you realize that the words you chose were not the right words—you were never the person they suggested you were; now let's say that there is a loaded gun in the house and you toy with the idea of using it and say, "Go ahead, shoot yourself," but here, too, the words are not right, so, as you have often done, you revise them before it's too late.

A LETTER FROM TEGUCIGALPA

Dear Henrietta, since you were kind enough to ask why I no longer write, I shall do my best to answer you. In the old days, my thoughts like tiny sparks would flare up in the almost dark of consciousness and I would transcribe them, and page after page shone with a light that I called my own. I would sit at my desk amazed by what had just happened. And even as I watched the lights fade and my thoughts become small, meaningless memorials in the afterglow of so much promise, I was still amazed. And when they disappeared, as they inevitably did, I was ready to begin again, ready to sit in the dark for hours and wait for even a single spark, though I knew it would shed almost no light at all. What I had not realized then, but now know only too well, is that sparks carry within them the wish to be relieved of the burden of brightness. And that is why I no longer write, and why the dark is my freedom and my happiness.

MYSTERY AND SOLITUDE IN TOPEKA

Afternoon darkens into evening. A man falls deeper and deeper into the slow spiral of sleep, into the drift of it, the length of it, through what feels like mist, and comes at last to an open door through which he passes without knowing why, then again without knowing why goes to a room where he sits and waits while the room seems to close around him and the dark is darker than any he has known, and he feels something forming within him without being sure what it is, its hold on him growing, as if a story were about to unfold, in which two characters, Pleasure and Pain, commit the same crime, the one that is his, that he will confess to again and again, until it means nothing.

THERE WAS NOTHING TO BE DONE

Sorrow was everywhere. People on street corners would suddenly weep. They could not help themselves. In dark apartments, in parked cars, at roadside tables, people wept. The dog by his master's side, the cat on the sill, they wept as well. The king and the queen had died and so had the prince, and the president of the republic, and the stars of the silver screen. The whole world wept. And the weeping went round and round and could not stop.

NO WORDS CAN DESCRIBE IT

How those fires burned that are no longer, how the weather worsened, how the shadow of the seagull vanished without a trace. Was it the end of a season, the end of a life? Was it so long ago it seems it might never have been? What is it in us that lives in the past and longs for the future, or lives in the future and longs for the past? And what does it matter when light enters the room where a child sleeps and the waking mother, opening her eyes, wishes more than anything to be unwakened by what she cannot name?

IN THE AFTERLIFE

She stood beside me for years, or was it a moment? I cannot remember. Maybe I loved her, maybe I didn't. There was a house, and then no house. There were trees, but none remain. When no one remembers, what is there? You, whose moments are gone, who drift like smoke in the afterlife, tell me something, tell me anything.

FUTILITY IN KEY WEST

I was stretched out on the couch, about to doze off, when I imagined a small figure asleep on a couch identical to mine. "Wake up, little man, wake up," I cried. "The one you're waiting for is rising from the sea, wrapped in spume, and soon will come ashore. Beneath her feet the melancholy garden will turn bright green and the breezes will be light as babies' breath. Wake up, before this creature of the deep is gone and everything goes blank as sleep." How hard I try to wake the little man, how hard he sleeps. And the one who rose from the sea, her moment gone, how hard she has become—how hard those burning eyes, that burning hair.

ON THE HIDDEN BEAUTY OF MY SICKNESS

Whenever I thought of my sickness I would hear the melancholy sound of a viola. When I described it to the doctor, he heard the same sound. "You should keep your sickness to yourself," he said. One cloudless summer day, I went outside; some crows gathered around me and were silent. I took this as a tribute to the hidden beauty of my sickness. When I told the doctor, he said, "Your sickness may be catching and could ruin everything. Therefore, I am no longer your doctor." Yesterday, when I considered my sickness, I saw my parents, naked in the baking heat, kissing and whispering. I was worried where my sickness was leading me, and turned my attention to a distant town, to its golden clock, its white stone villas, its boulevards crowded with angels shielding their eyes from the sun.

WITH ONLY THE STARS TO GUIDE US

Whenever the giants turned in for the night, taking their huge toys with them, we were left nothing to play with, and slept under sofas and chairs. The gift of bigness would never be ours. This was a truth against which we had tried again and again to turn our tiny backs, and each time had failed. Undone by sorrow, some of us found solace in prayer, and others, like ourselves, chose to follow wild dogs through the dark, moose-crowded woods of the northland, nursing their hurt until they dropped.

TROUBLE IN POCATELLO

It was autumn. It was late in the day. A storm was coming. Flocks of birds were flying south. A pink-and-purple sunset stained the house, the wind gusted, branches tossed, leaves dropped like dead moths on a sisal rug. "I'm home," said the husband. "Not again," said the wife.

LIKE A LEAF CARRIED OFF BY THE WIND

After leaving work, where he is not known and where his job is a mystery even to himself, he walks down dimly lit streets and dark alleys to his room at the other end of town in the rear of a run-down apartment house. It is winter and he walks hunched over with the collar of his coat turned up. When he gets to his room, he sits at a small table and looks at the book open before him. Its pages are blank, which is why he is able to gaze at them for hours.

THE SOCIAL WORKER AND THE MONKEY

Once I sat in a room with a monkey who told me he was not a monkey. I understood his anguish at being trapped in a body he detested. "Sir," I said, "I think I know what you are feeling, and I would like to help you." "Treat me like a monkey," he said. "It serves me right."

NOBODY KNOWS WHAT IS KNOWN

A man and a woman were on a train. The man said, "Are we going someplace? I don't think so, not this time. This is already the next century, and look where we are. Nowhere. Tell me, Gwendolyn, when we boarded the train, why hadn't we known this day would come?" "Snap out of it," Gwendolyn said. The train was crossing an endless snow-covered plain; no town awaited its arrival, no town lamented its departure. It simply kept going, and that was its purpose—to slither dreamlike over blank stretches of country, issuing sorrowful wails that would slowly fade in the cold.

THOSE LITTLE LEGS AND AWFUL HANDS

Night had fallen. A man who was staying at the Grand Hotel walked to the beach, lit a cigar, opened a black umbrella, and leaned back in a canvas beach chair, holding the cigar in one hand and the umbrella in the other. I wanted to ask him, why the umbrella, but I was too timid. Then, I heard him say, "Those little legs and awful hands, will I never be rid of them?" I patted my legs, then looked at my hands, and knew that he had not meant me, and certainly not himself, but maybe another, someone he might have hated, or even loved. But down the beach, a woman, wearing very large mittens, was coming toward him, rapidly, with baby steps. He jumped up from the beach chair, tossed his cigar, and with his umbrella began to run; he ran and ran, trying to escape, as if he could ever escape.

NOT TO MISS THE GREAT THING

It was to happen. He knew it would happen. He would have secret knowledge of when that would be, and be there early to welcome it. The gates to the city were closed. A cloud lowered itself into the central square and disappeared into an unmarked alley. A large woman with sequins in her hair studied him from a distance. A cold rain fell on all the houses but his. Suddenly it stopped, and he walked out into the yellow light. "Maybe it's come," he thought, "maybe this is it, maybe this is all it is."

NOCTURNE OF THE POET WHO LOVED THE MOON

I have grown tired of the moon, tired of its look of astonishment, the blue ice of its gaze, its arrivals and departures, of the way it gathers lovers and loners under its invisible wings, failing to distinguish between them. I have grown tired of so much that used to entrance me, tired of watching cloud shadows pass over sunlit grass, of seeing swans glide back and forth across the lake, of peering into the dark, hoping to find an image of a self as yet unborn. Let plainness enter the eye, plainness like a table on which nothing is set, like a table that is not yet even a table.

IN THE GRAND BALLROOM OF THE NEW ETERNITY

They sway like drunks in delirious exile from sense, letting their blindness guide them ever further from what might have been theirs, letting their former selves fade and be lost in the dusk of forgetfulness, never to be regained, never to be more than an idea of once having been, so that the light which had been theirs is gone for good. And when the doctors come, it is too late. The shades above the city have already been drawn, the pockets of wind have been emptied.

WHEN I TURNED A HUNDRED

I wanted to go on an immense journey, to travel night and day into the unknown until, forgetting my old self, I came into possession of a new self, one that I might have missed on my previous travels. But the first step was beyond me. I lay in bed, unable to move, pondering, as one does at my age, the ways of melancholy—how it seeps into the spirit, how it disincarnates the will, how it banishes the senses to the chill of twilight, how even the best and worst intentions wither in its keep. I kept staring at the ceiling, then suddenly felt a blast of cold air, and I was gone.

Notes and Acknowledgments

I would like to thank my editor, Deborah Garrison, for her kindness, understanding, and help over the years; and Caroline Zancan and Annie Eggers, who have been, at different times, her assistant editors.

Sources of the quotations used in The Monument *are listed here by section and in the order in which they appear in each section.*

2 "The Old Poem" by Octavio Paz. From *Eagle or Sun?,* translated by Eliot Weinberger. Copyright © 1976 by Octavio Paz and Eliot Weinberger. Reprinted by permission of New Directions Publishing Corporation.

3 "The Secret of Life" by Miguel de Unamuno. From *The Agony of Christianity and Essays on Faith,* translated by Anthony Kerrigan. Copyright © 1974 by Princeton University Press. Volume 5 of *The Selected Works of Miguel de Unamuno,* Bollingen Series LXXXV. Reprinted by permission.

"Nuances of a Theme by Williams" by Wallace Stevens. From *The Collected Poems of Wallace Stevens.* Copyright © 1923, renewed 1951 by Wallace Stevens. Reprinted by permission of Alfred A. Knopf, Inc.

4 Sonnet Number 3 by William Shakespeare.

"Letter to a Friend" by Sir Thomas Browne. From *The Prose of Sir Thomas Browne.* W. W. Norton and Company, Inc., 1972.

"The Secret of Life" by Miguel de Unamuno.

6 *The Seagull* by Anton Chekhov.

"Thus Spoke Zarathustra" by Friedrich Nietzsche. From *The Portable*

Nietzsche, translated by Walter Kaufmann. Copyright © 1954 by The Viking Press, Inc. Reprinted by permission.

"To a Little Girl, One Year Old, in a Ruined Fortress" by Robert Penn Warren. From *Selected Poems 1923–1975.* Copyright © 1955 by Robert Penn Warren. Reprinted by permission of Random House, Inc.

8 Sonnet Number 101 by William Shakespeare.

9 "The Man with the Blue Guitar" by Wallace Stevens. From *The Collected Poems of Wallace Stevens.* Copyright © 1936 by Wallace Stevens. Renewed 1964 by Holly Stevens. Reprinted by permission of Alfred A. Knopf, Inc.

15 "Hydriotaphia or Urne Buriall" by Sir Thomas Browne.

18 "Song of Myself" by Walt Whitman.

"I Am Not I" by Juan Ramon Jimenez. From *Forty Poems of Juan Ramon Jimenez,* translated by Robert Bly. Copyright © 1967 by The Sixties Press. Reprinted by permission of The Seventies Press.

In Praise of Darkness by Jorge Luis Borges, translated by Norman Thomas di Giovanni. Copyright © 1969, 1970, 1971, 1972, 1973, 1974 by Emece Editores S. A. and Norman Thomas di Giovanni. Reprinted by permission of E. P. Dutton & Company, Inc.

19 "Death Is a Dream" by M. Playa.

21 *The Fall into Time* by E. M. Cioran, translated by Richard Howard. Copyright © 1964 Editions Gallimard, translation Copyright © 1970 Quadrangle Books. Reprinted by permission.

22 "The Twelve Caesars (Nero)" by Suetonius. From *Suetonius,* translated by Robert Graves. Copyright © 1957 by Robert Graves. Reprinted by permission of Allen Lane, The Penguin Press.

25 *Edmond Jaloux* by Yanette Deletang-Tardif.

30 "The Prelude" (Book XIII) by William Wordsworth.
The Gospel According to St. Mark, 13.37.

37 "Essay upon Epitaphs" by William Wordsworth.
"Letter to a Friend" by Sir Thomas Browne.

38 "Sad Strains of a Gay Waltz" by Wallace Stevens. From *The Col-*

lected Poems of Wallace Stevens. Copyright © 1936 by Wallace
Stevens. Renewed 1964 by Holly Stevens. Reprinted by permis-
sion of Alfred A. Knopf, Inc.

47 "Spin from Your Entrails" by Miguel de Unamuno. From *The Agony
of Christianity and Essays on Faith,* translated by Anthony Ker-
rigan. Copyright © 1974 by Princeton University Press. Volume
5 of *The Selected Works of Miguel de Unamuno,* Bollingen Series
LXXXXV. Reprinted by permission.

"A Noiseless Patient Spider" by Walt Whitman.

50 Anonymous Greek poem, translated by W. H. D. Rouse. From
An Anthology of Greek Poetry in Translation. Copyright © 1937
by W. H. D. Rouse. Reprinted by permission of Oxford University
Press.

"Hydriotaphia or Urne Buriall" by Sir Thomas Browne.

52 *Thus Spoke Zarathustra* by Friedrich Nietzsche.

"O Living Always, Always Dying" by Walt Whitman.

The following dedications and notes for the volume Dark Harbor *are
listed here by section.*

x   *is for Jacqueline Osherow.*

xii   *is for Ann E. Waters.*

xiii   *is for Jorie Graham.*

xvi   *is for Brooke Hopkins. The someone alluded to is Wallace Stevens.*

xviii   *The quotation is from Rilke's poem "Lament."*

xxv   *is for Richard Howard.*

xxviii   *The someone quoted is John Ashbery.*

xxxiii   *"In the mirror the body becomes simultaneously visible and untouch-
able" is from Octavio Paz.*

xxxiv   *The quotation is from William Wordsworth.*

xliii   *"The Lament of the Pianos Heard in Rich Neighborhoods" is a poem
by Jules Laforgue. "Piano Practice at the Academy of the Holy
Angels" is a poem by Wallace Stevens.*

Index of Titles

A NOTE ON THE TYPE

This book was set in Celeste, a typeface created in 1994 by the designer Chris Burke. He describes it as a modern, humanistic face having less contrast between thick and thin strokes than other modern types such as Bodoni, Didot, and Walbaum. Tempered by some old-style traits and with a contemporary, slightly modular letterspacing, Celeste is highly readable and especially adapted for current digital printing processes which render an increasingly exacting letterform.

Composed by North Market Street Graphics,
Lancaster, Pennsylvania

Printed and bound by Berryville Graphics,
Berryville, Virginia